A PENGUIN SPECIAL

FROM A SPANISH JAIL

EVA FOREST

FROM A SPANISH JAIL

Translated by Rosemary Sheed

PENGUIN BOOKS

Penguin Books Ltd, Harmondsworth, Middlesex, England
Penguin Books Inc., 7110 Ambassador Road, Baltimore, Maryland 21207, U.S.A.
Penguin Books Australia Ltd, Ringwood, Victoria, Australia
Penguin Books Canada Ltd, 41 Steelcase Road West, Markham, Ontario, Canada
Penguin Books (N.Z.) Ltd,
182–190 Wairau Road, Auckland 10, New Zealand

—

First published by Éditions des femmes 1975
English translation published in Penguin Books 1975

—

Copyright © Éditions des femmes, 1975
This translation copyright © Rosemary Sheed, 1975

—

Made and printed in Great Britain
by Richard Clay (The Chaucer Press), Ltd,
Bungay, Suffolk
Set in Linotype Pilgrim

I dedicate this book – but why name names when the witch-hunt is still going on, and people can be questioned simply because they are friends of ours? I dedicate it to *them all*, and in particular to my friends Reme, Mari Luz and Encarna, with whom I share a cell and a great many other things, and who have withstood this injustice with so much dignity. I also dedicate it to my lawyer Juan María Bandrés, who has shown courage in times of difficulty, and has from the first brought so much human warmth to our defence.

CONTENTS

PUBLISHER'S NOTE

On 28 April this year the Spanish government declared a 'state of exception' in the Basque provinces of Vizcaya and Guipuzcoa. During the summer months an estimated 16,000 police and a counter-insurgency force of 900 men have been drafted to the North. The government's action is in response to the bombings, killings of policemen, strikes and general unrest which is particularly associated with the ETA, the Basque revolutionary movement. These kinds of disturbances are by no means confined to the North. Strikes and demonstrations are increasingly commonplace in a country where the question which obsesses everyone is 'After Franco – what?'

There is no freedom of political association in Spain and hundreds of men and women are in jail for their opposition to General Franco's ruling National Movement. These include communists, socialists, liberals, trade-union leaders, priests, students and members of the professions. 'Offences against the State' are tried in the special courts, The Tribunales de Orden Público, which have been set up to deal with political crimes. Convictions are often made on the flimsiest evidence or from statements extracted under torture. It is against this background that the case of Genoveva Forest *et al.* must be considered.

On 13 September 1974, a bomb exploded in the Café Rolando in the Puerta del Sol in Madrid. Twelve people were killed and some seventy injured. The Café Rolando is known to be frequented by the Brigada Político-Social (BPS), the Spanish political police force, whose headquarters, the notorious Dirección de Seguridad Social, lies near by. The police blamed the militant wing of the ETA, ETA V for the crime. As far as is known, the only evidence they had for this supposition was given to them by José María Arruabarrena who, with José Antonio

Garmendia, was arrested on 28 August 1974. The events surrounding these two men, and indeed the whole affair, are shrouded in secrecy. However, it appears that Arruabarrena, who was shot in the leg at the time of his arrest, was to be transferred from hospital in San Sebastian to Madrid on 13 September. En route, he was suddenly taken to another hospital where he went into a deep sleep. He awoke three days later to find the police in possession of a statement, apparently made by himself, to the effect that a group of intellectuals, artists and workers had been constructing hiding-places (*refugios*) in their homes.

Within the next few days a number of people were arrested, among them Genoveva Forest, Antonio Durán (a worker), Lidia Falcó (a lawyer and leading feminist) and Mari Luz Fernández (a teacher).[1] In all, five of the people arrested were women. Apart from the fact that they were all friends, it is difficult to imagine why this group of people should have been selected rather than any other.

Comparing the dates of all these events, one is struck by the coincidence between them. September 13: the café is bombed in Madrid and Arruabarrena is moved towards Madrid; September 16: Arruabarrena's 'statement' is in the hands of the police and the first arrests are made. A Reuters dispatch of the following October sheds interesting light on the affair. It revealed that a notice had been posted in the DGS just before the bombing, warning personnel to keep away from the café.

Eva Forest, the author of this journal *From a Spanish Jail* is very well-known in the intellectual circles of Madrid. As a doctor of psychiatric medicine, she works in a psychiatric collective and is a founder member of the MDM, the Democratic Women's Movement. Her husband, Alfonso Sastre, is an internationally known dramatist whose entire literary career has been dogged by the censor. Eva Forest is herself the author of a work on her experiences on a Cuban farm.

On 16 September, three days after the Puerta del Sol explosion, Eva Forest was taken from her home to the DGS where

---

1. A letter from Mari Luz Fernández is included in this book, p. 185.

she was held illegally for nine days. Under Spanish law, a prisoner may only be held for seventy-two hours by the police. He must then either be freed or handed over to the judiciary. Beatings, insults, threats to her children and tales of the torture and even the death of her husband followed. In fact Alfonso Sastre was not in custody until the first week of October when he gave himself up to the judicial authorities, no doubt fearing ill-treatment from the police should they manage to capture him. He was subsequently released on bail.

Eva Forest was transferred to Yeserías, the women's prison in Madrid, where she was kept incommunicado for another nineteen days. The only clue as to what she or any of those arrested with her were to be accused of was the press release by José Sainz, head of the BPS. Sainz declared that those arrested were known communists and members of the ETA. This statement aroused considerable scepticism as it is well-known that the political positions of the two movements are incompatible – the Communist Party of Spain has followed a non-violent, reformist line since 1948.

Since her incarceration, Eva Forest has been subjected to rigorous interrogations by the prosecution. It gradually became clear that she was to be indicted not only with complicity in the Café Rolando affair, but also in the murder of Carrero Blanco, the Spanish Prime Minister and successor designate to Franco. The ETA had claimed responsibility for Carrero Blanco's death in a bomb attack in December 1973 but have always vigorously denied any connection with the Café Rolando killings.

In political cases, such as Eva Forest's, the prosecution has developed a cat-and-mouse technique of refusing to name dates for trials to open, or setting them and then switching them around thereby obstructing preparation of the defence. It is still not known when Eva Forest's trial will take place. Nor is it known conclusively whether she will be tried under the Public Order Law in the Tribunal de Orden Público or, as is very likely in a military court. The possibility of a summary trial by the military is a cause for grave concern as the nature of the accusations may lead the prosecution to ask for the death penalty which Spanish military law would require to be carried out within twelve hours either by firing squad or by the *garrote vil* (strangulation).

The letters in this book were written from prison to her three children, Juan aged eighteen, a medical student in Cuba, Pablo aged sixteen and Eva aged twelve. The journal with which the book opens was written during seven days of her solitary confinement at the prison. As the dates in the journal show, Eva is clearly confused when she says that she wrote it in five days. Mari Luz Fernández, whose letter to her lawyer is included near the end of the book, was kept in solitary confinement for over 100 days in appalling conditions. Dressed only in the light summer clothes she had been wearing at the time of her arrest, she was denied even a bar of soap to wash with. Like Eva Forest she was badly tortured. It was not until prisoners at Carabanchel and Yeserías threatened to go on hunger strike that her confinement was ended.

PROLOGUE

No he de callar por más que con el dedo,
ya tocando la boca, ya la frente,
silencio avises o amenaces miedo . . .[1]

(FRANCISCO DE QUEVEDO, 1580–1645)

When it was suggested to me a few days ago that this book be published, my first reaction was to say No. Not just because it is not the aggressive book I have it in me to write and would like to write *now*, but also because these are intimate letters, never intended to be read by other eyes, and written in a crisis situation of which all I now remember is the immense effort I had to make to overcome it and carry on. *Carry on in spite of everything*, so that one day I could express it; so that there would remain some evidence of that time of hallucination which still leaves me blind and shattered. For months these letters represented my sole hope amid the madness that lay all round us and which we were forced to become part of; they were my way of clutching onto a solid and dearly loved reality. They were rather like a regular appointment not to be missed, a pleasurable duty, an engagement which helped to keep up my morale however bad things were.

All this was certainly something far too personal to consider letting it be published as it stood. Hence my first refusal. But then I thought it over again carefully, in view of the situation.

---

1. 'I will not keep silent, however much you admonish me to be quiet and try to frighten me, with your finger on your lips or your forehead ...' Francisco de Quevedo was a prolific writer of prose and poetry and was deeply involved in politics. He suffered imprisonment because of his writings and has had a profound influence on subsequent generations including the present one. [Ed.]

It is not a unique situation, but one that is all too familiar to those who have been as concerned as we have with solidarity over the years. And I could not help realizing how much support might be given now by such a document – a testament, simply a straightforward letter reiterating a warning call and helping people to understand what is happening. It was this that overcame my resistance. If someone wants to publish this book as a valuable tool that might contribute to the struggle we are all engaged in, then I accept its publication with pleasure. The book is now with the publishers and they can do what they think best with it. I have no corrections to make, and there is no point in my re-reading it. I know that my children, to whom the letters really belong, will support my decision. They were no longer private anyhow, once they had been opened to undergo the double censorship of the prison authorities and the military.

This, then, is an *ad hoc* book, a book with a purpose: it is to draw attention to a collective problem; in short, it is a *book of solidarity*. It is this purpose that gives it its true value, and only in this sense that it should be read. To read it in any other light would be to distort its meaning. To the extent that it fulfils this aim, I am in full support of its publication, and I am tremendously grateful to my comrades in the 'Politique et Psychanalyse' group who have shown such warm solidarity from the first, and have spared no energy in their defence of us. Words cannot describe the emotion I felt on reading – through the glass of the visiting room, misted over by our breath, or perhaps by my own tears – the petition they published in *Le Monde*.[2] It was one of the first whispers of hope to get through to us from outside.

---

2. This account of events and statement of solidarity, having been rejected and censored by the press, had to be published as a paid advertisement in *Le Monde*, 23 October 1974, by the women who first signed it. It was afterwards signed by thousands of women in different countries, and published in a special issue of the *Quotidien des femmes*, 23 November 1974, directed to making more widely known the revolutionary struggle going on in Spain. This special

From the day of the first press conference given by the Head of the Security Service, which was reported widely by the news media all over the country, we have been overwhelmed with hostile comments, lies, and calumnies. From time to time, mass-circulation publications like the magazine *Meridiano 2000*, or the book *Puerta del Sol 2.30*, disregarding the most elementary moral principles, present information received from highly dubious sources as though it were gospel truth, and we are put in serious danger. It has been said of me that I have strange hypnotic powers, that I can control people from a distance, that I exercise an evil influence on those around me. So horrific are the things that are said, that merely for people to read this book and discover that I am not a monster with two heads breathing fire, and that I have a human heart beating inside me like everyone else, is in itself a major step forward.

But the real problem is neither so obvious nor so recent; it has lain beneath the surface for years, at once far more profound and far less grotesque : in the strictest sense, it is a tragedy. One day people will be able to understand more clearly the complexity of the situation we are living through now, and the significance of the vengeance that is breaking over our heads today. They will also understand the intellectual poverty we have been reduced to, which has prevented our saying what we had to say publicly, and which has scarred us so deeply. I am thinking especially of my husband Alfonso Sastre, who has been in prison for over five months for having written a letter of protest. It is painful to compare that with the now historic letter sent by Sartre to the Military Tribunal during the Algerian war of liberation. Now, as then, many of us would like to be able to say what we too feel – that we are ready to 'carry the luggage' of our comrades fighting for a just cause. But what would elsewhere be a basic proclamation of dignity becomes here a crime so serious as to involve its author in a Kafka-esque trial at law. I have sadly to recognize that, in one way or another, we have always had to act in secrecy; and I

issue was written collectively by some Spanish women, and the women in the French 'Politics and Psychoanalysis' group.

am anxious as an intellectual, from my prison, to declare my protest. That is perhaps why I have decided today to sign my name to this prologue, which seems to transform it into a commitment.

They have said they would also like me to say something about myself ...

I hardly know what to say. That a large part of my life is involved with the history of my people, and that we have often witnessed and indeed taken part in unforgettable events? That one morning, for instance, we were beaten simply for taking red flowers to the funeral of Pedro Patiño, a building worker who had been shot for trying to defend his rights? That we were also beaten, though more seriously, for denouncing the tortures inflicted on the Asturian miners? That we were chased through the streets of Baeza like dogs when we tried to pay our homage to Antonio Machado, a poet of the people? That there were hideous threats when we at the University described violent confrontations in which we had been involved? That they have always done everything they could to trample us into the ground? Perhaps that is why our hearts bleed whenever a worker – in San Adrián del Besos or Vigo, in Grenada or Bilbao – is shot merely for claiming what is his by right. Should I say how profoundly I love all the peoples who make up the Spanish nation, with all their human wealth of unachieved potential? That – even if it is dangerous – I will not conceal the fact that I have Basque friends who dream one day of finding a solution to 'the Basque problem'? Or that my conscience pains me over Puig Antich, as a brother we did not help enough, whom we let them kill one day at dawn? How terrible that was ...

I want to say that I have always felt a sense of solidarity with all the condemned and exploited of the earth, even though it took the death of a Bolivian guerrilla to determine my commitment, in full realization of the consequences. That the struggles of the Vietnamese people and the Palestinian people are examples we follow closely. That I support struggles for liberation everywhere. That I wept bitterly over the Chilean 11 September. And that I have had moments of great joy – such as the day when as a united people we saved Angela Davis, whose struggle was our own, and the day when the Portuguese prisoners who were our friends were set free.

I want to say that where there is injustice I feel a vast and terrible anger surging within me. That perhaps it is rooted in my childhood – in my memories of children being machine-gunned by great black aeroplanes in a fishing district of red Barcelona. That my father was probably a great-hearted anarchist, and that my mother is as brave as any old lady in the Vietnamese NLF – I can pay her no higher compliment.

I should like to say that the problem of revolution is always in the forefront of my mind. That I support the liberation of women in all its aspects, and that I believe that not until they get political power will they be able to begin their own much-needed revolution.

These are the matters that fill my mind, the things I should like to talk about at leisure. I have presented them here all higgledy-piggledy, from notes which now lie in a pile on the desk of some Military Judge, and may even be used as evidence in fearsome accusations.

But ultimately these are just little things in one person's life, and their real importance is that they are part of the lives of *all* of us, and that they make up the history of our people. What matters is that we, here, are wide awake; we are really interested in what is happening in the rest of the world. And from the rest of the world a wave of warm feeling comes to us, teaching us yet again that Solidarity really matters: Peter Weiss is not just a writer who lives in Stockholm, nor is Gisèle Halimi just a lawyer with cases to plead, nor is Fernando Arrabal just an avant-garde writer of successful plays. There is a great common force uniting us with all our good friends in Portugal, Italy, Japan, Scandinavia, the United States, Cuba, and everywhere else: our dream of a better world where a human being can really be a human being.

Let me say it again: it is our solidarity that makes us strong; so strong that today, in our corner here, our island-battlefield of Yeserías, we can look forward to the future optimistically, sending you our love: and with it we enclose this poem sent to us by another comrade in another prison:

> *Pero a pesar de todos los procesos*
> *la noche es enemiga, nuestro el día:*
> *nosotros somos libres y ellos presos.*[3]

March 1975   EVA FOREST

---

3. 'Despite all the lawsuits, the night is the enemy's, the day is ours: it's we who are free, and they who are prisoners.'

JOURNAL

My dear children,

I am beginning this kind of letter–journal late in the afternoon of 29 September,[1] on this day the Military Authority in
charge of my case has let me have a ballpoint and a few sheets
of paper – a special favour for someone in solitary confinement.

I start by telling you this so that you may know that ever
since being transferred to this prison my one thought has been
to find out what's happening to you; I'm *longing* to talk to
you, and I've millions of things to tell you about what has
happened in the past few days ... Only the past few days,
because I don't really want to talk about the nine days I spent
in the basement of the DGS. Not yet, anyway. It's not that I
want to hide anything from you – I trust you, and you know
I never lie to you. But today I don't feel strong enough to
think about it. However I can at least tell you that I'm not
sorry to have had the experience; it taught me a lot. It's given
me material for an article on psychology, and a very good
article on the problem I've been concerned with lately – anti-
psychiatry. I think I might even make some notes that could
be worked up into a play – I have the strangest feeling of having lived through a series of short playlets, like flashes, all set
against a complicated décor in my own mind, and each leading
into the next. I've made some notes for it – it would be in

---

1. French editor's note: This diary was written by Eva between
29 September and 5 October 1974, in Yeserías Prison in Madrid,
where she was in solitary confinement. She had just come from
spending nine days at the Dirección General de Seguridad (DGS).

seventeen tableaux, for each scene has been vividly etched in my memory during recent events. Perhaps I'll end up competing with your father!

What I'd really like to do is to file that bit of the past away for a while, and just tell you about my time here – where, all things considered, life isn't too bad. My cell is quite big enough for me on my own; the paint is fresh, and it is very clean and light. (One wall consists almost entirely of translucent glass.) When I first came in, I burst into tears – it seemed like heaven.

Coming from the DGS, a real Dante's Inferno, I was in the kind of super-sensitive state when you really appreciate comfort and warmth – like some mornings when I got back from long and painful interrogations, when I used to curl up on the mattress in my cell and warm my hands – and the rest of me – by taking little sips of coffee (nastier coffee than most people would normally drink!). My wrists would still be hurting from the terribly tight handcuffs.

I wasn't going to talk about that, but it will keep coming up – perhaps it's better that way.

When they did bring me up from the basement, they were very rough. While they were putting back into my bag the things which they had taken out of it, they put me in a corner with my arms handcuffed behind me, to make me as uncomfortable as possible. Then they slung my bag round my neck, hanging down on my chest, and pushed me and pulled me, insulting me as we went, till they'd dragged me into the daylight, in the DGS courtyard. There they shoved me into a Black Maria. The journey was both terrifying and absurd – a good example of what your father defines as 'multi-level tragedy' – I mean that it was all so grotesque and at the same time so overwhelming that I didn't know whether to laugh or cry. I'll have to admit that I was mostly nearer laughing. What a lot could be said about one's complexity of feeling in extreme situations! I felt like a kind of motorized Servetus.[2]

The drive was indescribable. There were three policemen

2. Michael Servetus was denounced by Calvin as a heretic, taken through the streets and burnt at the stake in 1553. [Ed.]

covering me with machine-guns in the back of the van, and two more in the cab with the driver – they were taking no chances! There was one jeep with a full crew in front of us, and another behind. Both with sirens and blue lights. So we set off – and the journey was quite eventful. The guards swore at one another. The driver of the van swore at the jeep-drivers for losing the way – in the end they went the wrong way down a one-way street and blocked up all the traffic! Being right at the back, all I could see was that we went through every red light, and our sirens can't have been loud enough, because we kept almost hitting other vehicles. We finally got to the prison, and they put me into the cell I've been telling you about.

It really is very comfortable. I've got a bed with a proper mattress, a bedside table and a rug. On the lower shelf of the table are my plates, which are filled with (appetizing) food for lunch and supper, and a glass which I can fill from the tap – and though Madrid water is far from pure, it is one of the best-tasting city waters I know. The reason I'm saying all this is that you all know the importance I attach to this subject, and how fussy I am about the need for a balanced diet. Well, we really have one here. So you needn't worry about bringing me anything. The food is nice, and varied, and I don't need any extras. Perhaps later on, when I'm out of solitary confinement, I'll ask you for some coffee – you know my weakness for that ... And when I'm living in a more normal way I'll ask for some clothes. I'm still wearing the same black and white striped blouse (it's worn so thin you can almost see through it) and cotton trousers I had on the day they arrested me – which was of course *hot*. I haven't been able to change; the day I got here I was very dirty, and they had to lend me a grey smock (which is what the women prisoners here wear) while I washed my own clothes. So, when I'm allowed to, I'll ask you for a few of the things I'm having to manage without – but I'll tell you when the time comes. The main thing is that I am very well physically (you always knew I was as strong as a horse); as for my spirits, I am generally pretty cheerful, though at times I feel rather low. My four days on my own here have given me a chance to think and meditate, and I've really appreciated having *time* – something you don't get in the bustle of ordinary life. As long as I can read and write, I don't think a short period completely alone will be a wholly bad thing ...

At the moment my room is all lit up by the sunset, and it makes me feel rather melancholy. There are so many things I want to say, and I don't know where to begin. But never mind, I expect this chat will develop in its own way. I don't want to hurry – so much has happened to me that I think it would be too much for you to describe it all at once. In fact I think I'd really rather not recall what has happened in the recent past, because it is still too painful. Perhaps I'll be able to tell you about it all quite calmly one day. I don't even know whether you'll ever be able to read this diary; it may never get to you. But I know that for me it is a kind of lifeline. I'm writing and writing, almost without a pause, terrified of empty hours. I believe that if I hadn't been able to write I should have died of despair. However ...

One thing: from now on I shall be writing to all three of you, so please make a photocopy of all my letters, and send them on to Juan (short of my writing it all over again, that is the only way he can share in all this with you). You won't forget, will you?

One thing that worries me a lot is the continuity – the rhythm – of your lives. Life must go on, for all our sakes and especially for mine, in my present situation. If I can know that you are studying as you have always done, going on with your languages, keeping up your swimming – that your education is continuing normally, in other words – then I'll have the courage to work and study and write, too ... What has happened is a misfortune in all our lives; one day I'll be able to explain it to you properly – we'll have a lot of talking to catch up on. I can't ask you not to let it affect you – obviously it is a terrible shock, and you can't help feeling miserable, but you must get over it somehow and carry on. Eva darling, do you remember my telling you that there is an answer to everything? What is happening to us now, however awful you find it, *will have* an answer. Our family is so united (and not all families are), and you will find we are soon all together again, sitting chatting round the white kitchen table where we used to have our meals.

So, cheer up! You, Pablo, must do well in your studies – you've done so brilliantly up to now. I presume you have passed the University entrance exam? Poor boy, you didn't exactly have the best conditions for taking it in! I keep thinking how hard it must have been to sit an exam with so much trouble on your mind. The reason I asked you to go away during the search was because I thought the best thing was for life to go on – even though I didn't then realize what terrible accusations they were going to make against me : I thought up to the last moment that it was just an administrative formality that would be settled in a few hours. Poor Pablo! I'm still wondering whether you passed your exam, or whether you even got there to take it ... Did you go on to enrol in the department of languages? Are you writing? And my little Eva – so loving, so intelligent, so lively – has she started the new school year happily?

I don't yet know how my life here will be organized, but I'm hoping to see you once a week, if possible and if it's safe for you (I rather think there are two visiting day a week, but I don't want you to lose too much studying time; you must just come once, and we can write to each other), and then we can talk over all the various problems. For we need to talk more than ever now – just as I said to Juan in my letters after he left (and I am saying it to him again now, since this letter is to him as well!). We *must* be able to tell one another everything ... Lately, lying in bed, I have sometimes laughed to think that Juan and I are now *both* studying at the public expense! And I've sometimes thought: How strange Tío Maroma's[3] family is – the further separated we are, the more

---

3. 'Tío Maroma's family' is the nickname used of themselves by the family. Spanish-speaking people commonly use nicknames within the family, which are not normally used in the presence of outsiders. This particular name refers to a nineteenth century *sainete* or one-act farce (a very popular form of theatre in Spain and Latin America) in which there is a family – *la familia del Tío*

united we become. (Remember how we felt that when Juan went?) So you see, I can still laugh. You must never lose the ability to laugh either; if you keep a sense of humour, you keep your sensitivity and your critical sense, and the combination of those two things helps people to survive a lot without becoming embittered. I hope you're listening, Eva, my merry Mafaldita,[4] my baby growing up so fast, my poppet.

I wish I could write your father a long letter to tell him all that I feel for him, and how dreadful it has been thinking that I may have been the cause of all he is now going through. I haven't managed to get any detailed news of his situation: they told me he was in prison, that he tried to escape when they were arresting him, that he was wounded and that his condition was serious ... Then they laughed and contradicted this, and said that he had escaped – which made me think that his condition must be very serious indeed ... But we can talk about this when I am allowed visitors ... For the moment, please, if you do see him, talk to him on the phone, or write to him, tell him that it is impossible to love anyone more than I love him, and that I can only say how terribly sorry I am that I acted so impulsively and without more forethought. I wait and long for the day I can hold him again in my arms. If you only knew how much he was in my mind in those nights at the DGS; honestly, I used to hear his voice in the distance, and hear him moaning, and hear such strange things ... Then for hours I would make great efforts to communicate with him – by God knows what wild notions of telepathy I thought it possible – to convince him that he must escape, that he mustn't let them capture him in the street, that I could put up with any amount of suffering if only I knew he was free, and looking after you, and that I was the only one to be going through all this.

Maroma – who are very simple, loving and united and who become plunged against their will into all sorts of sophisticated complications. [Translator].

4. French editor's note: Mafalda is the little-girl heroine of a strip cartoon by the Argentinian humorist Quino.

Eva darling, it is night-time now, and they will be putting out my light at ten, as usual: the wardress comes and switches it off from outside, leaving us in the dark till the morning. I keep thinking of you; I can see your little face, your soft eyes which are so deep and sometimes have a look of fear in them as though the whole of you were in some strange anguish. I feel very close to you; I'm watching you, and I cannot bear you ever to say, 'I'm not very happy.' I mean it, Eva; you must *never* give way to thoughts like that – if black moods come, you must make a great effort and shake them off. I want you to be merry and to sing; I like to remember you singing as you did your homework, your history and arithmetic and grammar; or, long ago, when you used to rock yourself to sleep singing. I am thinking about you now, and I love you; I send all my love to you, and to my great tall Juan, and to my smiling, dreamy Pablo.

And as I still have a few minutes – Pablo, my slim and supple, and sometimes so thoughtful future writer of dreams and realities – don't waste time tormenting yourself on my account. Our lives – the lives of all of us who belong to this large and peculiar family of Tío Maroma – are very rich and, through all our wisdom *and* all our foolishness, always very human. And you can be sure that whatever happens to us can only make us closer. Tonight I am feeling very proud of you all: the more I think about you, the more extraordinary you are. And I'm proud of you, Juan, so far and yet so near. and longing to hug you – you need affection so much, and do you realize it is over a year since I've put my arms round you? You're the future doctor of a new kind of medicine, and you will be a great man. And quickly, before I go to bed, for it's only a matter of seconds, a final kiss for your father – a perfect companion as well as the greatest love of my life (a life made rich and happy by learning from him how to achieve freedom).

... There are still a few minutes left – I can hear things happening some way off so the wardress won't be here for a while ... I've had supper and put away my plates for to-morrow, and I'm in bed. There is so much I want to know. I really *need* to know it in order to keep my feet on the ground – to know definite facts and not lose myself in unreal dreams. What are you all reading? What films have you seen? What problems are worrying you? What was the last nice thing you did? What has made you unhappy, apart from our separation? Tell me everything. I need to know – and I'll tell you what I'm reading and what I'm worrying about too ... Yesterday I read the *Iliad* (of all things!) and two very interesting short works by Colette, whose writing I know very little of. One, *La Vagabonde*, is about the life of a theatre-café actress, and I think Papa would love it, and so would all of you. It's not much, but they were the only two books to be found in the entire prison, because they're in the process of moving, and there's no library yet. Good night ...

COMMENTS

(It is interesting to analyse this first day of the diary – my fourth in the new situation. In spite of having arrived in a state of emotional shock, it shows no evidence of intense nervousness. There is more a sense of clutching at normal life, wanting everything to be as it was before; things must go on, plans must be made for the future. It seems like an attempt to shut my eyes and retreat into a cosy shell, as though I were saying: 'I must go forward and leave the past behind, for nothing can alter it. What matters now is to get away from that and carry on.'

I don't show the least concern over what people – people I am fond of – outside may be thinking. It is as though nothing had happened in their lives at all, as though they had stayed fixed in the position they were in when I left. I give no thought to the anguish they may be feeling, the changes that may have happened. Reality is distorted by the most powerful subjectivism. For everyone else things are just the same. Of course, this diary was written in one of my worst moments – just after coming from being tortured. Just after making my first statements to the Military Authority. It gives the impression that, even though I was thinking of all that had happened, and was taking it into account, I did not really

understand the magnitude of it all, and felt a kind of mean-
ingless happiness that was resolutely superficial – or possibly
a way of not becoming ill? Also, there must have been a whole
– conscious and unconscious – mechanism at work to prevent
my saying anything I was not supposed to say, starting with
the very fact that there were things I was not supposed to say.
All those things are excluded from the first. This text was
written in the knowledge that every word would be read by
the Military Authority.)

In the past few days I have been thinking a lot about the
imagination, and I'm only sorry I didn't put my ideas down on
paper – but I'll do it bit by bit. Some of them may be of some
use to Alfonso, for his study of 'The dialectical imagination'.
(That is a *very* important book, and he must not on any
account give it up!) It is a problem I keep thinking about. I
can't get over the thought of all the years he has been working on it, and now, just as he seemed to be able to give all
his time to it and the end seemed in sight, this has to happen to
interrupt him. Can he go on with it? He must realize that the
book has got to be finished quickly, and published as soon as
possible. I think perhaps this is the thing I am most concerned
about. I had a very strange experience connected with it. One
of the times when they were torturing me, as I came round
after fainting for the second time, after some very sharply
defined feelings which I'll describe later on, I suddenly saw
very clearly what imagination means to me: 'Imagination is
what is possible' (though that possibility may not yet exist,
and may take centuries to eventuate). And I could have written
a long dissertation on the subject. (The only thing that stopped
me was not having the time.) It was a strange phenomenon –
as though having got beyond the capacity to feel but basing
myself on it all the same, I had made a leap to a high level of
understanding, and was reflecting better and more clearly than
ever before upon the synthesis of my long-garnered experience ... Perhaps this all sounds a bit complicated – at least to
you, Eva, because Pablo and Juan and I have often talked
about this sort of thing, and I know you two will understand

... Anyhow, I am also writing for Alfonso's benefit. Will you be able to see him soon? Are you seeing him? I dare not ask any more questions. I only hope this journal gets to you ...

Forgive this messy letter. I'm writing on my knees, and there's nothing to rest the paper on. Not many consumer durables here! ... My worldly goods amount to one cake of soap, one comb, one toothbrush, the blue pencil I'm writing with, a packet of cigarettes and a box of matches ... I haven't even got my own towel. In the solitary-confinement section, there is a very threadbare communal towel which I approach with some caution, as it is used by so many people who are passing through – but the other day I managed to wash it ... If I want to change my clothes, I have to stay in bed with nothing on while mine dry ... which I did the other day, after my shower. Oh, I haven't mentioned the shower! It was so lovely being able to use it the day I got here. I had come from the DGS (sorry to keep bringing in the DGS, but things keep happening that remind me of that time) ... I was almost black. (If you could have *seen* the water – it looked as though all the dye had run out of my clothes!) I was exhausted and filthy, my hair was disgusting and my nails were long and claw-like. That first bath was a real soothing embrace!

I said I was finding it hard to write, with nothing to lean on ... I've just had breakfast, and put away my bowl. So now I'm ready to tell you a bit more. I've taken to dreaming a lot the past few nights – strange depressing dreams, with a lot of breaks in them, which I find it very hard to remember; so I make a real effort to set about reconstructing them – a bit like really interesting jigsaw puzzles. Heaven knows what's going on in my subconscious all the time! So many things must be knocking about down there, full of all the really profound truth I dare not face! What clever defence mechanisms we have!

One of my dreams – the day before yesterday – was marvellous; at least the part I'm going to tell you. It was a very long and complicated dream, and extremely symbolic; I remember it very well because it was so clear when I woke up.

I was quite near home, by the Ampliación area, and I went

into a shop to buy some shoes. (Do you remember going with me a little while ago to Galerías to buy shoes, Alfonso?) I needed some tough shoes for a lot of walking, but they showed me some very dressy ones, elegant, furry, fantastic white ones. I don't know why, because they weren't the kind of thing I like, in fact they were rather vulgar, but I was delighted with them and put them on. I don't remember the next part of the dream, but then I was on the Garraf coast, by the beach, walking in a very rugged area with lots of caves. I can remember there being cliffs, and I think the train went that way. Then, someone who was walking along with some other people came up to me and said: 'Don't you think your shoes are a bit unsuitable for this place?' I realized that was true, and took them off. I took them off one after the other very carefully, because they were so white and soft and feathery. I shook them because the toes were all muddy, and then the toes moved and became two little heads, and the shoes turned into two beautiful white doves. I laid them together in the shoe-box and carefully made some tiny holes in the lid. 'These shoes must breathe,' I said to myself. Then, I put the box under my arm and started to walk – and I saw myself in a kind of Chaplinesque film – getting further off and smaller as I walked slowly away. Isn't that a lovely dream? Lovely, and symbolic. Anyway, I hope you like it; and perhaps Pablo can write a story round it.

It's a bit cool this morning, and it's quite true that my clothes aren't warm enough. This afternoon I'll ask the Prosecutor if I can be lent a jacket. I haven't told you much about him; his name is Herrero, and he is the military interrogator who is preparing the case. So he isn't actually the Prosecutor, but the person who prepares the indictment. I think this is the first civilian case he has handled, because his normal work is with military trials inside the Army. In fact I get the feeling that it has come on him as something of a thunderbolt. He hasn't paused since the 17th. He goes through the events very intensely, and seems racked by doubt and suspicion ... He is extremely conscientious, and analyses everything in the most minute detail – so his interrogations are endless. I have spent hours and hours talking to him. Sometimes we start in the late afternoon and don't finish till one or two in the morning. He must be quite exhausted – though not as much as I am, because on top of it all I am being kept shut up here and have no idea how long it's going on for ... Today I got terribly mixed up, but this isn't the time to tell you about the indictment because it's all very hush-hush, and if I do I'm afraid they won't let this journal out. It's all very complicated ...

I'm thinking about you, Pablo, starting at the University. I'm so afraid something may happen to you. I know you're sensible and will keep out of trouble, but you can't be too careful. Work hard, but only go there when you absolutely have to, and do as much as you can at home. It would be too awful if anything happened to you, when you have so much to cope with, with Eva, and me, and everything else. Don't be in too much of a hurry. Only with real accurate knowledge can one come to understand anything, and above all, to know what one wants. Please don't think I'm giving you the usual maternal advice. I've always told you that what matters is to *know*, so that you can choose, and that that sort of knowledge can't be skimped. I'm telling you not to get into trouble at the moment just because I hope you will one day *know enough* to make the right, *informed* decision ... But I must stop. This is sounding like when I used to say, 'Have you washed your ears?' (I trust, by the way, that you do wash them sometimes?!)

At this time of the morning there is a silence in my cell that is quite peaceful ... In the afternoon it is heavier and more depressing; but now, if only I had a typewriter, I would sit down and write some of the endless things I've planned for which I've never had time. I much regret that the book on 'The life of a tinker and other instructive lives' never got beyond the planning stage. (What happened to those tapes? What happened to all the other things that must be lost by now? We had some really splendid material collected for that ...) Perhaps Pablo will feel like taking it up, and typing it all out ... It should be done, you know, because there might really be a chance of getting it published at this moment ... Anyway, we'll work something out ... (I'm noting down on a separate bit of paper a large number of things that need doing, and that you must deal with if you possibly can.)

And Juan – what is he doing at present? I've been thinking of him a great deal just now, perhaps because it's so long since I've heard anything ... I'd like to know the syllabus of that second year of medicine so I can stick my oar in! What practical work are you doing this year? I presume you have become quite an expert in public health. I can put up with a lot, and our separation isn't half as painful, when I think how you are making such good progress – and that all of you are going on, one way or another, enriching your lives with something you really enjoy. What about you, Pablo? You realize you can do what Juan is doing if you want to – but I should think you're all right here for the moment. If you've got into the University, that is a good beginning. You'll know what you want in time ...

Today I'm going to tell you something funny: I would have you know that, small as it is, I always go for a walk in my cell, first thing in the morning, and again before going to bed. It keeps me in condition. The first day I worked out how long my steps are, and concluded that 150 steps is more or less equivalent to 100 metres. So, I reckon I walk two kilometres or more per day. In the morning, I get out of bed and set off. Sometimes, when I'm thirsty, I stop by the *Palomas* fountain (i.e. the white plastic jug on my bedside table, which I've called after the doves in my dream). By the end I feel so fit that I do some gymnastic exercises. Then back to my reading, or writing – or sleeping. There's not much to do in a tiny cell like this!

But I don't get bored, I promise you. In the afternoon, the light comes in in little golden triangles through the panes of the window (each pane is fifteen centimetres by twenty, and they open), and as the sun gets lower, they change shape – getting longer, and wider, splitting in two when one of the little metal divisions casts a shadow. It's intriguing; makes me think of the cubists and their re-composition of forms. It also makes me think of geometry, and calculating areas, and all sorts of things linked with that ... It's fascinating. When the first of the three triangles reaches the door, the glow of the wood makes golden reflections all over the room. That's the last act. Then it gets dark and they put the lights on – if they remember: sometimes they forget, and then we're left almost in the dark for quite some time. That is actually very pleasant ... Sometimes there's a voice to break the monotony, a shout from one of the 'recluses' as they are called here. Yesterday a woman began shouting. The wardresses told me afterwards that she's twenty-nine, and a prostitute; she is brought in pretty regularly almost every month, and then transferred to the psychiatric section. She banged on the door because they'd locked her in, and the way she shouted sounded mad, but what she was saying was really quite sane. It reminded me of my student days, when I used to visit and work in mental hospitals. I spent a long time recalling my 'traditional' psychiatric knowledge, and thinking how it all needs to be thought out again; we need a new approach to all those problems. I think that when they let me read what I want you must bring me all the Laing books we have. Will you try to remember that in case I forget to ask? Another thing I'm going to need is a fine ball-point – it's quite hard to write with the kind they sell here. In fact I could really do with a fountain pen ... A pen was what I used in Cuba, when I was writing that endlessly long book which has never yet been published. A pen has happy associations – *and* my handwriting is better with one ... It is odd how much physical pleasure I get from writing by hand. But I need a typewriter too, for making the first draft – more because I find the feeling in my fingers stimulating (it has a wonderful effect, almost as though life were somehow being transmitted to your mind by way of your hands) than for convenience ... Then I have to make corrections, re-write, make notes in the margin, take it to bits and put it together again ... (Writing is really a very peculiar activity!)

At the beginning, when I had no paper or books, I used to smoke a little – six cigarettes or so, no more, because I was always determined to keep very fit and healthy, and absorb no toxic substances (which is why I never take pills, either). But now the packet is on my table, with two cigarettes teasing me which I shan't ever smoke. I hope you're listening, Pablo? And you, Juan – but it's a long time since you've said anything about smoking in your letters, so I hope you have given up that bad habit.

I am suddenly reminded of the profound sensation I had on one of the occasions when I passed out in the DGS. It's very hard to explain: a sudden switch from feeling good to feeling bad ... You know how normally, when you're dreaming something horrible, and you wake up, you feel delighted because it was only a dream. Well, I did it the other way round. I remember, I was on the floor, and there was a moment, just as I was beginning to come to, when I couldn't yet see but I could hear: the blood was pulsing in my ears, and I had a feeling of being alive, and for a moment I thought, 'How marvellous, it was all a dream!', and I felt happier than words can say – absolutely *saturated* with pleasure ... Then, a second later, when my sight returned, and I began seeing their huge shadows above me, bending over, and I was back in the miserable reality of the torture room, I was filled with such desolation as I had never, ever felt. It was a few minutes after that that I thought that thing I mentioned before, about the Imagination being a leap onto another level ... Does that make sense? I'm telling you this now, because it has just come into my mind – not to distress you. I am absolutely all right now, and I think it is right that you should know about it though you mustn't worry about it, because it is all over: we can talk about it and learn something from it, and that's what matters.

It seems to me now that the Imagination is a kind of motor – that it moves, and it moves other things. It is what collects up the accumulation of past experience, and changes it into new forms, and 'dynamizes' it and propels it into the future. If life were only what is past it would stop being alive – it would be a useless memory, a kind of card index or a mammoth filing brain. It's the combination of all those memories – all that 'data' – that extends horizons and opens new fields of investigation. And combining the data of the past with those of the present, of the here and now of every day, is the dialectical work of the imagination. Imagination is a bit like energy in physics, changing all the time, creating new possibilities, opening endless fields of investigation. A life without imagination would not be a *human* life: it is the capacity to imagine that characterizes an intelligent being. What would intelligence be without it? Even mathematical knowledge – as I came to realize during those days when I was killing time by working out mathematical problems – is simply a concoction made *by imagination* out of real facts; in most cases (at least for those of us who aren't mathematically minded) the answers have already been discovered by other people – though there's always a possibility of finding something new.

(Two pages are missing here, in which I worked out some ideas about the imagination; I copied them out in a letter to Alfonso, and then by mistake destroyed them.)

Have I mentioned that I've got a friend? A fly. It was quite chilly outside yesterday, and it slipped in through one of the open panes at the top of the window. I watched it come in. I was lying on my back, watching the light, and suddenly it came whizzing in and settled on the little triangle of sun on the wall. Very sensible – it's just where I'd have gone myself if I was that size! I was very annoyed at first – you know how I hate insects anyway, and this one seemed particularly intrusive, coming to disturb my own particular moment of peace. I got up and tried to drive it out again. I chased it for over an hour, hunting it with a sheet of paper, and shaking my bedspread at it. But it just laughed at me and stayed where it was.

Its determination not to go out in the cold finally won my heart. I can't stroke flies with my fingers like Pablo (or any of the other friendly things his fertile imagination would have suggested), so I resigned myself to leaving it alone. It must have been grateful in its own way, because it didn't bother me at all. It followed the contours of the wall from one patch of sun to another, giving little jumps, then staying still for a bit, then investigating the terrain a bit more. This went on till they put the light on. It looked very pleased with itself – perhaps it really was grateful ... But when the light came on – it's a huge, dim, depressing round thing – I watched the little creature fly round looking quite disconcerted, and finally after a long tour, it settled on the slippery glass. When they brought my supper, it must have been able to smell the food or something, because it flew down and settled on my knee, beside the steaming plate. I gently pushed it away, meaning to say, 'No; this is mine, but I'll leave you a bit,' but it became quite cheeky, and I had to be severe. I don't know if it was sad, or angry or resentful, but it flew off and I didn't see it again. This morning we woke up at the same time. Our relationship is excellent, and I think we shall be quite happy together. It appears to be an independent kind of fly, something of an anarchist, and it must have some rudimentary intelligence, because you don't have to tell it anything more than once. It seems to have grasped that we each keep to our own territory, and respect each other's rights. To tell the truth, I am beginning to feel quite fond of it . . . I suppose it's not surprising.

To go on about imagination : I was wondering a moment ago how far imagination is possible without reality. The imagination needs knowledge, something to work from; it has to start with facts that are either here and now, or from the past but still in the memory. To imagine things, I have to consider the past and relate it to the present reality surrounding me. And the more of both that I have (experience and knowledge from the past and knowledge of the present) the richer the process of relating the two will be. In other words, this brings me back to the question of intelligence. If I think dialectically, then I am thinking better, because I am understanding the full complexity of the reality around me. But this form of knowledge – of associating past and present – though it's a necessary step, is not itself the step I make when I create, or research, or discover : that is something I can only do when I *go on from* all that to imagine what more might be possible.

If you think about the area Alfonso is dealing with in his work, imagining a work of fiction is one means of finding a way into reality, and thereby entering into it and changing it. But I still feel that the question of knowledge is terribly important. If my data from the past and the present are accurate, and correspond to the reality, then my imagination will be building upon a really solid base, and will be intervening in reality in a rational way; therefore it will be a continuation of advancing knowledge. (I'm still thinking of fiction.) If you start with Snow White, for instance, or Puss-in-Boots, you obviously never get anywhere, because you're bounded by a circle of fantasy from which there's no way out (thought it's perfectly real in one's imagination, because that is how things happen there). This is the world of the symbolic, of the reality or surreality of dreams, of an endless variety of games – but not very much else. At most it's an exploration of forms, or of shadows, but with data that are confused and not properly understood. To get out of that circle you have to break out, and get through to face reality ... I think it's true what Alfonso says – that the dialectical imagination is reality (was that how he put it?). I think there *is* no imagination apart from reality – at least in its full, complex sense. The problem is identifying the bounds of that reality.

Really, reality is everything. The thing is that there is reality that can be verified, that can be stated in scientific terms, and there is also reality that can't be verified, and is absurd (?). What are the criteria for deciding where one stops and the other begins? And when does today's absurdity become tomorrow's possibility?

It has just struck me that there was a play on TV last Friday – could it have been *La Mordaza*? It was the interrogator, I think, who told me it was due to be shown that day. It's ironical how for *years* Spanish TV has never shown any of Alfonso's work, and now, the first time it happens, things have to be like this!...

I keep asking you questions, all through this journal, which you'll probably never see. This isn't an order – but I would like you to answer them. For instance: Juan, did you get the last lot of books I sent? We tried to choose whatever we could find that related to Spanish history to help you build up a library on the subject, since it interests you so much. I hope you've seen Milagros and Arturo. I'm sorry not to have been there when they came back, to hear what they had to say about it all, and about all you're doing. But Pablo, my golden-eyed, blond messenger, will go back and forth and deliver your (much longed-for) letters to me. Now more than ever I wish I had a recent photo of you. And, speaking of photos, do you know that at the beginning, when I was first here, I spread out all the photos I always carry in my wallet. (And I'm so glad I had them – I must have had a presentiment!) I laid them all out on the bed together, like a display in a shop window, and began thinking back to the time each one was taken; I went into the story of each one, and it was like reading so many really good novels. I must say that there are some of Alfonso I was sorry not to have, and one of Juan with his arms round me – the last time I saw those was on the desk of a policeman who was questioning me; they must have kept them after they'd checked my wallet. I suppose I ought to demand them back, as a matter of principle, but I feel too weary ... so many monstrous things have happened recently that it seems almost silly to get annoyed about a thing like this ... But it really does make me very angry. You know how little things can mount up?

Anyhow, let me tell you, after looking at all your portraits for so long, you all seem to me very beautiful indeed, – and that includes Yaya.[5] I've never really seen you quite so well before, at once so near and so far (i.e. both affectionately and objectively!) – and you are fantastic. You really are beautiful, and I've spent hours looking at you!

Juan, I've suddenly remembered that when you went to the Ministry to get your passport last summer they couldn't find it. You must keep on at them. It would be awful to lose it, especially now when anything might happen, and you might have to come home at short notice. You must get it sorted out, and the sooner the better. I should think Pepe and Anisia could help you, because they know how the administration works better than you do. *Don't* just leave it!

If the imagination starts off from data (I mean data that can be scientifically verified), then the things imagined will be verifiable too. In other words, if, starting off from real data I were to imagine producing a particular bridge, or a building, a

---

5. French editor's note: The nickname of Eva's mother.

play or a mathematical discovery, that product of my imagination could be converted into a verifiable reality – something that could go on in its turn to serve as the basis and reference for further investigations by the imagination. I think I'm beginning to have an idea of just what it is that I understand by imagination: what is imagined is what *can* be verified or implemented (though it hasn't yet been). In other words, it is the *potential for development that things have within them*. (Perhaps what has no potential development in it, but only goes round in aimless circles, should be called fantasy?) Hence the tremendous power of the imagination, its immense potential, when the data it is working on are accurate. It seems to me that that is the way modern mathematics is advancing – not that I know anything about mathematics! – and indeed I would go so far as to say that it is the only way science can possibly advance: lassoing the future, as it were, with its imagination. We all have examples of this in everyday life: things we have previously imagined which become possible because they have been thought out on a logical basis ... Everything that is possible is possible. That sounds like a truism. But the imagination *is* the possible. The more I think about this, the more convinced I am of it. The rest is fantasy ...

Certainly there are boundaries to the sphere of the imagination, but it is hard to pinpoint them. Hard to know how far what seems impossible today will one day become possible. (My mind turns to Jules Verne, but that's not really a helpful example.) In the field of fiction that Alfonso is studying, this could be anything from the most realistic school of novels to science fiction.

How I wish I could be talking about Alfonso's book now. It's a really *great* book that he's writing! It was tremendously exciting reading the first chapters of it in the summer. Ever since I was arrested I've been haunted by the thought that it may never be finished. Perhaps that explains why it was in my very worst moments that I tended to find myself thinking about the subject. I had a kind of will to carry on, to make sure that nothing in the world should stop him finishing; it was as if something inside me was saying, almost without my realizing it, 'If he stops you must carry on, you must take it up, it mustn't be left unfinished.' Perhaps that explains that strange experience I had when I came to on the floor in the DGS?

It's evening again. Somewhere in the distance a clock has just struck eight. I think it's supper time in the other buildings, but we get our food brought a bit later. It's already pretty dark. I shall sit here in the twilight till they come and turn the light on : a door will open some way off, then someone will come down the corridor, and turn on the central switch, and the light in my ceiling will come on. But it's nice sitting thinking in the dark, remembering things. I have a very strange feeling ... I am in Yeserías and the name seems to mean something to me – I've heard it before some time, long ago, but when? I think it was Tere who used to tell us things about the time after the war, and about men being herded in here for a long period of waiting that meant eventual death ... Wasn't Yeserías once a hospital? even perhaps quite recently? I've lost all sense of time and space. Yeserías seems like a far-away island, I don't know where, and something once happened here, but I don't know when ... I think they used to come in every day – in the morning, I think they said, with a long list which they read out one by one ... And apparently the people used to go out singing, almost joking about it; some of them sang that song, 'La Pepa es una gachí ...' [6] A fine acting-out of what Alfonso calls multi-level tragedy. Ridiculing death ... Ours is a great people, cast in a heroic mould ... And now, all these years afterwards, I've landed up here, in Yeserías – a building filled with history, and solidarity, and fraternity ... As I look at the newly-painted walls of this newly-painted building, I hear the echo of all those voices around me – comforting me and making me feel braver. I'm sure experience gets passed on somehow, and what is really important remains – but how do you get hold of it? How can you tell the world all that's happened here, and all that's happening still? Oh dear, they're coming with the dinner trolley – just as I was beginning to recover from the confused state I've been in since I was arrested! Never mind, don't worry. This old hospital-cum-

---

6. 'The death sentence is a gorgeous girl'.

prison is quite a light and cheerful place now, with the walls all white and the doors in light wood ... I'm so glad they've brought me here and not somewhere else.

I'm worried about Yaya. I know there's been a lot about all this in the newspapers. (I could see that from the reaction of the *grises*[7] at the DGS when they were threatening to kill me, and saying they'd shoot me as a murderer, etc. What the papers said must have been really terrible!) and I wonder how she has stood up to the ghastliness of it. I only hope you'd rung her up and warned her. But she's old and she's not strong, and I do worry about what all this will do to her. What's the best thing to do? Once the house is in order again – from what I heard at the DGS I imagine it must have been pretty well gutted – she'd be all right in Madrid; she could come for a good long visit, and she'd feel really useful. (It's terribly important to feel useful when you're old!) And old people like Yaya, who aren't caught up in the toils of the world, have such a lot to teach ... And Yaya has always been so healthy and happy, and she's so shrewd and clear-headed ... I really do think she'd be well off in Madrid – but you will have to settle things as seems best to you. I've got a separate piece of paper, which the interrogator says I'll certainly be able to get out of here fairly soon, and I'm making a list on it of things you'll have to deal with.

And what about your other grandmother? I keep thinking how hard it is that all this should have happened to her when she was already so very depressed. She'll have seen things in the papers too – and on TV? – I can't find out exactly what they did say, but it must have been frightful. I hate to think how ashamed it must have made her ... A mother has such great hopes for her son! It must be terrible suddenly seeing on television what a monster his wife has turned out to be ... Obviously I don't need to tell you to explain it all to her, but it would be nice if you could see her. I'm not worried about the rest of the family – they're such wonderful people, and I

7. Member of the Brigada Político-Social, also popularly known as the 'Gristapo', because of the grey of their uniforms. [Ed.]

know they'll always stand by us. I realize more than ever now how much I love them and how completely I trust them. Actually, though I seem so communicative, I don't talk a lot about what I really feel inside. Give them all a great deal of love from me.

It occurs to me that all I'm doing is giving messages, and that the only person who can impart them is Pablo – my messenger with the straight blond hair and golden eyes. Don't worry too much about them, love. Concentrate on your work, and only deal with the most important ones when you find yourself with a bit of free time. Nothing is more important than for you to study hard and get ready for the future. And you do know that when I talk of studies I don't mean just exams, but the real work that will deepen your understanding of the world we live in.

I'm starting to write to you again today, the 1st of October. It's the middle of the morning, and I can't pretend to be in very good spirits. But it's quite natural – one's spirits go up and down like some kind of thermometer with every change in the atmosphere. I don't want to lie to you, so I must tell you that I've heard some bad news, which has alarmed me considerably, and made me even more anxious than I was already. I can't tell you much more, because I don't think I'd be allowed to, but it is about some of the people in my case. In fact, what is happening to us is a major catastrophe, and there's no telling where it will end. I feel as if some cataclysm has occurred, and we have *by no means* come to the end of the sufferings they have in store for us. I don't want to distress you too much, but I don't like writing to you without letting you share what's going on. Anyway, if you think Eva might be too upset, don't read her this paragraph. As if things weren't already bad enough, a new witness has appeared who can only be called insane. (I don't know what name to give to his particular mental sickness.) I can't say any more – except that there's been a tragedy inside one family which, in one way or another, affects every one of us. I can also tell you that it is reminiscent of Shakespeare. I've had to start my today's journal with this, because you'd soon have realized that it's all I can do not to cry ... But actually, I find that talking with you makes me feel better. Shakespeare was, among other things, a great dramatist; he had a fantastic, really deep understanding of human passions. You should really read him in depth. Juan, do you think you'll have the time and the opportunity? I think one can always make time, at least a little tiny bit! We can get his works for you. I say this to you specially, because I know that your time is terribly taken up with all you have to do – and it's wonderful that you've got such high marks for your work, as you told us in your last few letters – but you mustn't abandon everything else. For the thing that will do most to help enrich your chosen field of study is to enrich yourself culturally and gain a wider view of your problems. It's terribly important to develop one's capacity to feel; that's the way to come to understand life. And there's no better way of doing that than by way of art – through the evidence of what people have written, painted, etc. I know there are times, and you are living in one of them, when experts have to be trained as fast as possible because the progress of one's country depends on it, but one must always be mindful of the great danger of having specialists who are simply specialists and nothing else. We have always been against this kind of compartmentalization which is such a mutilation of the individual, and any good revolutionary must always be aware of the risk. Genuine research, in whatever field, is always based on an over-all conception of the world; and that comes only through knowing different sorts of things. It's terribly important to read, and write, and to make the absolute *most* of all the wealth of feeling and intellect we all have within us. In other words, to THINK. And today, I suppose because circumstances have chanced to bring Shakespeare into my mind, I feel I must say this to you very strongly: read him. The story they told me today – not in the gayest conditions: it was four in the morning, and I was being interrogated, etc. – was about a fratricide (Do you know that word, Eva? Pablo will explain it to you, in the understanding way he always teaches you things) and it made a dreadful impression on me – even though it was only a psychological fratricide. I can't say any more. But Eva, you too should start reading something by Shakespeare. I think you are old enough to understand some of his tragedies, and you would really love *A Midsummer Night's Dream*. There are several writers you should be getting to know. When you start reading something, it's very important to find out not just who the author is, but when that book was written, what was happening in the world at the time, what sort of person the author was, and a whole lot of things which will help you to understand other things ... Great writers like Shakespeare are important because they have managed to capture a moment of their age, or a moment in the life of certain people, and this can be far more illuminating than a lot of history books – most of which are so bad that they distort more than they inform. Reading them gives us experience that helps us to understand the world we are living in a lot better. Perhaps Pablo would have time to sit down with you for a while and read you one of the tragedies, like he used to read *El Lazarillo* and *El Buscón*[8] – do you remember how the two of you used to laugh?

It's so hard to write with this ballpoint that I don't know whether you'll be able to read my writing. When I look at the page I can hardly believe it *is* my writing. I'm sorry if you find it an effort to read this journal. I hope that in a few days they'll let me have my own things. (I still don't know why they haven't let me keep them. The interrogator spent a long time looking at them, and decided to give me different ones. Perhaps it was the foreign trademark – it was the pen Alfonso brought me from Sweden – that made them think there might be something inside! I really have no idea.)

It's now the middle of the afternoon. It's sunny, and there's a lot of light in my room – too much for my sore eyes; I'd prefer some shade. There's no point in concealing the fact that I've been crying a lot. After all it's as human to cry as it is to laugh – and I feel intensely human ... Things are happening that are utterly incomprehensible, and it's a great effort just to survive. I feel that Kafka's Trial was *nothing* to what they're doing to us here. But I'm determined not to go under; I'm

---

8. Two picaresque novels. *La Vida del Buscón* is by Quevedo.

doing my very best to make sense of the chaotic situation we are in. I tell myself to keep calm. First of all I must try to understand what is happening myself, and after that we'll see. I must try to outline the real situation, and I must try to see it as objectively as possible and not let myself get lost in the fog ... Yet as things are, the minute I set about trying to put events into order, I become totally lost. What exactly am I trying to put into order? I don't understand *anything* that is happening. What is the point of the whole affair? It's terrible to be so powerless. I'm finding it unbearable not being able to communicate with anyone. What do people outside think? What is *happening* in the world outside? I've heard no news since the day I was arrested. What have they said about us? Who else have they got in prison? From what I've gathered during the hours and hours of questioning, quite a number of people have been affected. I feel so helpless! I have to spend hours and hours being questioned about two or three things I know nothing about. Arms caches? Friends in the armed forces? Do I know of any conspiracy being hatched? Honestly, Kafka didn't know the half of it! If only I could describe some of it – one day, perhaps ... Will that day ever come? But anyhow, as I say, don't pay too much attention to all this; today's one of my bad days, the sort of day when I *wish*, instead of writing, that I could be with you all, and we could talk and talk ... It's the sort of day when you say to your nearest and dearest, 'Look, I'm not feeling too well today; I'd rather be left alone' – but there has to be *someone* to say it to!! You see what I mean, don't you? We've never kept things from each other, and that's why we've been so happy. Life is very complicated, and one can't just shut one's eyes to things. That's why I felt I should tell you about this bad time I've been through ... There are so many things I want to talk to you about, but then I don't know whether you'll ever actually see this journal; their letting me write it at all has been a tremendous concession.

It's now an hour later, and I want to let you know that the black clouds have lifted, and I'm feeling a lot better. A wardress has just come in with two books; I'm afraid they aren't very inspiring, but I'm quite ready to read them – they're a good distraction from the four walls of this room ... I'm beginning to understand that solitary confinement can develop into a subtle kind of torture ... I don't say that that's their intention in my case, but it's obvious that if you're left just to think and think for long enough you can end up in a state of complete non-being. I can see just how that would happen – it hasn't happened to me, but I'm afraid it may ... Four walls are terribly confining. Having no one to talk to is even more confining. If you have nothing to read and can't write, it becomes quite desperate. The time may well come when, in the absence of the dialectical interplay needed for thought, you end up as it were living on your own ideas, consuming yourself ... I don't really know. But I think that if I had nothing to read (and I have very little, because the library isn't in operation yet, so they can't bring me much) and if I had no paper, I could well become ill ...

It is seven in the evening. What are you all thinking about? What are you doing at this moment? I don't know how your day is organized, what your life is like, what people you see, whether you have been told anything, whether you're being harassed, whether Alfonso is in danger. I know nothing about *anything*. That's one of the things that makes me most miserable – not having any idea what is going on outside. I cling to the hope that everything is just as usual, but in my more lucid moments – moments of real misery – I know that things must have changed tremendously. But in what way? There's a kind of defence mechanism which blocks me from thinking too much about it. I spend most of the time in a kind of haze I can only describe as roseate which protects me from being fully awake ... Oh, how I wish you could come here! If only my solitary confinement would end, and we could have some kind of normal visiting and correspondence!

It's getting dark quite quickly now, and I'm writing almost in the dark. Outside I can hear people going back and forth collecting the dustbins – they're women, prisoners too, and they're shouting and joking and laughing. I feel quite ashamed of spending all these hours doing nothing every day, perhaps

thinking about quite unimportant things, or reading bad books
– when all of you are so weighed down with work and worry.
It's so frightful, this thing that's happened to us! But there's
nothing else I can do: I can only submerge in this submarine
of tedium, reading pointless books by Pereda and Ricardo León,
and try to survive. My problem is the exact opposite of yours:
I've got nothing to do, and you've got more than you can cope
with. The one thing we have in common is our longing for this
nightmare to finish soon, that and our tremendous love for
one another – something it's hard to find in this de-humanized
world we live in. Alfonso I keep close up against my heart, like
one of those stickers you used to stick in the alcove in the
kitchen – remember how furious I used to get with you because nothing, and nobody, could ever shift them?

I've had supper. I've smoked (!) my last cigarette of the day
– three today – and I'm about to go to bed and try to get to
sleep and make tomorrow come more quickly; that'll be the
2nd [October], and another today I'll somehow have to kill. I
send you all the love I've got in a great big hug. Good night
Eva, my little Mafalda, my poppet, my bundle of mischief,
with your darting eyes that see so deep ... Good night Pablo,
my young Pablo! – so sensible and dependable, and now suddenly the head of our scattered family – my beloved, dreamy
Pablo ... Good night Juan, far away in the Caribbean we all
love so much, my impassioned revolutionary, so curious about
everything; you've been away over a year now, my darling,
but it doesn't feel too bad because I know it really is for the
best ... Oh, how I love you all at this moment, as I say Good
night to you!

A little while ago, lying in my warm bed before I got up, I
was thinking that perhaps I'm writing too much, and this
flood of words will be one more burden, and take up too much
of your time which is already quite full enough ... But don't
worry; it's only for now. When my life becomes settled and
I get into a normal routine and have someone to talk to, a lot
of all this energy will escape through my mouth (not that I'm
such a great talker). Then I think you'll get a journal that's
less diffuse, and perhaps more worth reading. Now I just keep

writing and writing, mainly for something to do to fill up these *endless* hours. Solitary confinement is beginning to be a terrible strain. Especially since I don't know *what's* happening outside!

We'll have to make some arrangement about corresponding as soon as I'm allowed to write to you and get letters. I've already given some thought to it: you'll have to photocopy my letters and send them to Juan. And you'll somehow have to get his letters to me, or tell me what's in them. Then there'll be your letters – because I hope you'll write sometimes, even if we can see each other. And then there's Papa – after all he's the only real writer among the lot of us! And if this goes on for long, we'll need a filing cabinet for the 'Tío Maroma' correspondence.

I caught the wardress this morning when she came to wake us up, and managed to get her to let me have a shower. A shower is one of the very few pleasures there are in prison. I organized it very well. I still have nothing of my own – they've forbidden me to have any clothes or anything – but they left me a towel. It was a bit revolting, because it's used by everyone who comes in, and some of them are ill, but being all there was, I used it. I took the occasion to wash my trousers and shirt too; they were terribly dirty – you can imagine after all those days sleeping in that cellar, with all that filth and all the things they did to me! – and I put them to dry by the window. So I'm writing in bed, garbed in a kind of large striped shirt they've left me ... But I'm beautifully clean, and that's all that matters ...

I've written a few poems on another piece of paper, which I might send you as well – unless my critical sense forbids it!

No, to hell with them! I've torn them up. The best poem was the one you wrote by coming to visit me – everything seems pale and unreal in comparison to that. I wasn't expecting it. The interrogator had told me that you'd be allowed to come one day, but they've told me so many things ... When they called me I really thought I was dreaming. They'd closed up all the other buildings, and there was no one in sight in the passages or anywhere – I felt like someone very dangerous as I was being taken to the visiting room. Oh, how beautiful you are! I can't tell you how warm and happy I felt when I saw you. It was the first *real* thing I've felt for ages and ages! And you were smiling! Pablo especially – Eva looked to me rather more solemn. Your four eyes were dancing – they looked almost ready to jump out at me with all they wanted to say; and what a lot they did say – what a lot of love and happiness was there ... Perhaps Eva's not quite so much – I thought her smile was a little bit forced, as if she was doing her best not to let me see how worried she was. Darling Eva, we are terribly close, and there's nothing to worry about ... I wish I could set your mind at rest! I promise you that I really am very optimistic; I'm sure we shall be doing lots of things together again in the future, and that this nightmare will come to an end – the end will probably be just as ludicrous as the beginning. (I sometimes think it'll end like in that film, *Miracle in Milan*, when they all came out on broomsticks and flew up in the air – what's happening now is just as unbelievable!) I'm so happy, happier than I can possibly express in words – seeing you was absolutely overwhelming. You were warm like the sunshine, and so healthy, and alive, and innocent. You must have suffered such a lot all this time, and when you saw me your faces seemed somehow purified by emotion. I don't know why, but *never*, in all the time I've seen you and watched you, have I seen you looking so glorious. Your eyes absolutely devoured me, and you said so much that I'm going to have to spend a long time puzzling it all out, and thinking how to answer. Oh, it was so awful having only ten minutes! It went by in a flash – but it seemed somehow to have the intensity of a million light-years. I felt so many different things. I almost forgot that we were being watched – that the interrogator was behind you, and a wardress behind me, listening to everything we said. But it doesn't matter – I don't mind the world knowing how much we all love one another! And what about Alfonso? You weren't able to tell me much about him ... I gathered from Eva's lightning gesture that he's cut off his beard. Things must be pretty bad! Have the police really got him into a corner? How is he now? The poor darling! There

were so many things I had to say to you that I forgot half
of them ... But never mind. You've given me enough hope to
keep me going for quite a while. Your getting into the University is a great thing, Pablo. Life goes on, and you must carry
on as if nothing had happened. So, Pablo is at the School of
Journalism, and Eva is doing extremely well in the eighth
grade. We must somehow sort out the problem of your French
– you mustn't give it up this year and lose all the benefit of
that course you've had. That's good news about the Russian,
Pablo, that you can carry on your second year. You've sent me
an awful lot of money – I had 3,000 pesetas with me, and that
was ample – they don't let me buy anything here, because the
interrogator thinks I don't need anything. They now tell me
that you've left me another 5,000. That'll last me for a *year*
here! (Oh dear, I've written so much that my ballpoint's run
out ... I'll have to stop here and wait for them to bring me
another...)

I've been awake for some time, today, the 3rd of October,
but as they hadn't put the light on I stayed in bed. I didn't
get a fresh ballpoint till last night, so I couldn't write all the
millions of things I wanted to say to you. I really think that if
a time came when they stopped me writing this diary I couldn't
bear this solitary confinement any more. It's terribly hard being
locked up here without knowing what's going on in the outside world. From some of the things you said I gathered that
there's been a real wave of terror. I'm picturing the panic, the
anxiety, the uncertainty. What has been said about us? What
rumours? What lies? What's been said on the radio and television, and in the papers? What's come back to you about
me? And where is Alfonso hiding? (It seems clear that he *is*
hiding ...) It appals me to think of their catching him – I
couldn't bear to think of the police getting hold of him, after
all the cruelty and ferocity I witnessed. They seem to want
to make us the outlet for all their hatred, and I tremble to
think of him falling into their hands. Oh God, how can he save
himself? I'm back with the obsession that tormented me in
those last days in the DGS. He mustn't be caught. They mustn't
get him. They want to blame it all on him – but what is 'it all'?

That's the most terrifying thing – not even knowing what it is they are accusing us of. The only thing I know for sure is that THEY HATE US. All one can do is try to escape from such hatred, before they can visit it on us. I've heard all sorts of accusations made; they insulted me in every possible way in the DGS. It seemed a hatred that had been building up for a long time ... I know for certain that if they had had him then, they would have killed him. That was what I found most agonizing, hour after hour in my dungeon, whenever they let me rest for a while. I seemed to hear his voice coming at me from all directions, sometimes actually screaming and moaning. At other times, I could hear them taking down his description : Alfonso Sastre (...) writer ... It was terrible. Once I called out his name very loudly so that if he'd really been there he would have answered, and I'd have known we were together ... Now I'm again very much afraid this may happen. It might be better for him to go straight to the interrogator, and then there'd be no risk of him being picked up by the police. He must do something. Things can't go on like this.

It must be just past eight. A few minutes ago I heard a factory siren – it must be quite near here; it's a kind of siren I hadn't heard for years – I didn't think they used them in modern factories; it brings back all sorts of childhood memories, when we lived in Barcelona, and I used to hear them going off very early in the morning when I was still in bed. A whole wave of sensations – the factory, the strikes, my father talking excitedly about the workers' struggle and the terrible working conditions they had. It takes me back to those lovely Saturday mornings not so long ago (how long? two months – three – six?) when we used to read *Capital*, and almost wept over the descriptions of the oppressed proletariat in England when industrialization was at its height ... Do you remember, you inexperienced young things? This siren has a peculiar sound : it starts, becomes louder and more penetrating, continues for some time, and then gradually fades. It makes a kind of arc. In the war – that far off, legendary time you only know about by hearing us talk – it used to be the signal to take shelter. Now it sounds at eight, twelve, two and six. I keep thinking of my father: he was an anarchist with a great heart, and he painted most vividly the horrors of poverty in the poor parts of the city. I can almost see some of his pictures when I hear it: 'Women coming out of the factory', 'Dock workers', etc. When I get out of here – but where is 'here'? – I must explore the area and find out exactly where it is coming from, and what sort of factory it is ... I can't even imagine what part of town this is; it's obviously *in* the town – but that's all I know.

Now I hear them coming with breakfast. You know, I'm getting to be just like Yaya – I have my bowl of milky coffee, and dip my whole piece of bread in it, and you'd be amazed to see how much I enjoy it ... There now, I've finished!

I don't like re-reading what I've written, but I have a feeling that it is very monotonous and lifeless. I expect my physiological state affects it too – after all, think how ordinary menstruation can turn the world black! I mention this to help you see the way everything in life is linked with everything else; a human being is simply a complex combination of an infinity of things. And it can happen that without any change in his objective situation, he can see things one way one day, and quite differently the next. I'll stop now – I don't even feel like writing.

I spent yesterday feeling pretty rotten. Between these four walls, once one has gone through all the sounds, all the visible objects, and the other things I can see in my mind's eye, all one can do is think or sleep. I spend a great part of the time thinking, and I've found a good way of exercising my imagination by trying to get my ideas in order and consider how I am to face the future. I can see plenty of possible plans, but of course I can't decide on any one of them till my situation becomes a bit more stable. Most of them revolve round trying to see what kind of work I can do here. It's a fantastic effort not to let the time just slip by – or rather to fill it up in some way. I don't know if that is escapism – am I so afraid of what's going to happen that I don't even want to think of it? For over an hour I've been working out the entire plot of the picaresque novel I've had vaguely in mind for the past few years ... I really think I have perhaps got the kind of mind that sort of book needs – a critical sense, and a good sense of humour.

About all of you I don't know what to think. I know you're all right, that you're with friends, and that this terrible trial will soon be over. I'm sure you'll never want for understanding people to help you, or comrades to work with ... Until the other day I felt reassured at the thought that you were with Alfonso. Now, I realize more clearly how bad things are for him at present, and I don't know what to think. If he isn't around, then everything must be much more difficult.

Today is the 4th of October – a very special day. What a lot of memories it has in our history of Spain. I know how you love that history. Juan, did you get Tuñón's *History of the Workers' Movement*, and the other historical books we sent you? Remember that series of lectures you went to just before you left? A few days before I was arrested I saw some recently-published history books, and it struck me that that would be a good present to send you for your birthday. Pablo could buy them for me, if you'd like that?

On the 29th of this month it will be your glorious eighteenth birthday – being in your second year of medicine, and having done such a lot of other work as well, you're all set for a bright future. I wouldn't mind being a girl of that age, and being friends with you! By the way, how about Diana? You must tell us more about her – Oh dear! Don't pay too much attention to this kind of thing: I'm just being a typical mother! It really is hard to free oneself completely of that great weight of bourgeois ideology we are all burdened with ...

There's something a trifle absurd in my situation ... With all the complications and problems surrounding us, here I am lying on my bed, and all I can do is read a bad novel by Pereda. What a depressing way of killing time! I don't know which is worse – having nothing to read, or reading such nothing-books as this ... In spite of everything, though, I prefer this – it gives me a point of reference and makes me talk about something ... Seventeen days' solitary is a hell of a time, especially when I haven't the *least idea* what's been happening ...

A little while ago, I heard from the interrogator preparing

the case that Alfonso appeared before him yesterday – i.e. the 3rd of October – and after a brief interview went that same evening into Carabanchel prison; apparently that should mean that he'll be there a couple of days and then freed – provisionally. In other words, he's on trial too? I don't like the way this affair is going. But in a way – by what the interrogator told me – it's better for it to be like that. At least when he *is* set free, he knows he can't be detained by the police. He must have had a terrible time when he heard news of my death (suicide?) and other equally alarming and probable-sounding rumours; at least now he will have a few days' peace and quiet. I feel much better about him, but I'm worried about you – who's going to keep the family engine turning over now? You two little ones, my two poor little wretches, you've been left completely alone to cope with all the problems! I know there are friends and relations around, but that's not really enough. I've been spending this endless weekend thinking, and it seems to me a horrible situation for you. But you'll manage, and Papa will soon be back with you, and this time with a guarantee that he won't be taken away again – if there really *is* such a thing as a guarantee when it comes to the police. I'm in such an odd state of mind that I don't know whether it isn't better for him to be in prison – it's really strange.

Oh Pablo, what a lot of things I want to ask you, and what a lot of responsibility there is on your young shoulders! But you'll manage all right, I know. They've promised me that you'll be able to take your school-record in on Monday, and enrol at the University, so I hope that's what'll happen. And you'll soon have the keys of the house – poor old house, what a state it's in, with no windows, and holes in the walls, and all the books torn up and thrown about everywhere! I wonder how it'll be? It'll be a tremendous job to repair all that havoc, but you'll do it – and somehow we will all survive this horror. It'll be a great day when you come back to the house with Papa, and Yaya arrives! But as long as they keep me incommunicado we can't really start making plans ... There's so much you don't know what to do about – bank drafts, bills, publishers who owe us money ...

Eva darling, you'll have to take some of the responsibility in all this, too ... Your school work is the most important thing. But after that, you must try to make yourself useful where you are now – you've always been so practical and sensible, so you can certainly be a real help now ... Don't be too upset at having to do without things; everything will be all right soon, and you'll be back in your own little room – and you'll at last be able to use the lovely bag you chose in that little shop in Biarritz. What a strange name: 'Biarritz'! Odd to think that I had to undergo lengthy questioning – several times – because of having visited that pleasant little town. These days, travelling in the South of France seems to be a major crime. Having been in Biarritz seems to be irrefutable proof that I must know all sorts of things ... You'll have all your own clothes again and won't have to keep borrowing things – not that that's so very terrible.

I can't bear to think that you are alone tonight; nobody can ever make up for the *infinite* loneliness of knowing that the people you love most are in prison, and there are very few people, if any, to whom you can really describe your feelings. But I do think that it's only for a time. Eva darling, it'll be over soon. I'm longing to have you with me, and hear your voice – I wish I had one of your letters, or one of those marvellous little pictures of yours. And Juan – see how close we all are? Pablo told me the other day that he'd written to you three times. I'm so glad. You'll probably be getting all these sheaves of writing from me at the end of the month – the interrogator says I'll soon be allowed to send them out. They'll be a kind of small birthday present!

Pablo: I think when you go to photocopy all this to send it on to Juan, you'd better do it through Uncle Pepe, so you won't have to pay for it. We're going to have to economize more than ever now. Our precarious – and never very regular – income will go down with a bump – it would have to happen when were were already in debt, too ...

I can't *think*, if no information comes in from the outside world to stimulate my mind. My brain seems half asleep, and my ideas seem to be going round and round in ever decreasing circles. I feel that my brain is being affected by a restriction that could prove fatal – I think insanity must be something like that. I have a horrible fear that I may end up being what they call 'brainwashed' – that's what it feels like. You go on closing in more and more till a point comes when you are quite paralysed. That's what's happening – I feel as though I can't think because I'm paralysed. I can't even feel. I seem to be being rocked in a kind of haze that is de-sensitizing me; I'm somehow slowing down. Occasionally I make an effort to liven up; I get up and I start walking round the cell, like I did at the beginning – and I count my steps and try to get out of the morass I'm in. But it's terribly hard. Believe it or not, I actually *look forward* to when they come and interrogate me.

Today is the 5th of October ... It's funny how quickly *and* how slowly the time goes! I even got to the point of not wanting to write any more, because I'd given up all hope of these pages ever reaching you ... I'm still following the slow development of this case – but the trouble is that I'm not allowed to talk about it. I feel embroiled, and confused, and trapped; I work terribly hard to achieve nothing, making vain efforts to convince them of things they won't believe. There are times when I haven't even got the energy to defend my own beliefs. Something strange has happened to me in the last few interrogations, especially the very last one. Half way through I began feeling desperately sleepy – just after five o'clock, I should think – and I was dying to yawn, though I knew I shouldn't, but finally my sleepiness took over and I just let myself go – I seemed to be held in a kind of pleasant laziness, or weariness, or whatever. It's hardly surprising that I now hardly even hope this will ever get to you. It's almost as if I don't believe in anything any more unless I can actually see it. If I thought this were an ordinary correspondence that I knew would continue normally, I might feel spurred on to write, but as it is ... All through this past year, when I was writing to Juan, I knew the letters would take a week or two, but that he would get them in the end ... But this is all so *provisional* – like Alfonso's release: I've begun feeling that

that'll be delayed ... It's agonizing. I keep thinking of your father, still over there in Carabanchel, with no beard, worrying, lying on his back on his bed – like he used to in Miraflores – and I think perhaps he may be shivering with the cold, and I start shivering in sympathy ... I'm worried about his book. It really is a masterpiece, and it only needed one last burst of work to be finished. (Pablo, do tell the typist to guard the chapters she has like the apple of her eye – unless she's handed them back to you by now.) When Alfonso gets out, there'll be so many things he has to deal with that he may find it hard to get back to it, but he *must*! It's a book that must be finished as soon as possible. If you do everything you can to help him, he will be able to carry on. But of course I know you will. Another thing I'm concerned about is his University lectures in New York – has something been fixed about that? There are so many practical things like this that I want to know. I'm wondering if there's anyone who can give you a hand with all this. I hope my own situation will improve – then, even from in here, I could give you advice on all these practical points ...

In today's interrogation they gave me to understand that I shall see you again one day soon. Tomorrow, or the next day perhaps. If you only *knew* how I long to see you! I can't describe how I felt when I saw your eyes – begging for news about me and my situation, eyes bursting with questions! One day we'll be together again, and we'll go out into the country and have some really nice leisurely talks, like we used to do when we went for walks along the Canencia road on winter days. Eva: do you remember the time we went exploring in that forest where no one had ever been – except perhaps a wolf, because we saw some tracks – and found ourselves right at the top of Punta de la Pala? And Pablo, do you remember the day when we had that very serious talk and you asked me to explain to you about entropy? and schizophrenia? and there were a whole lot of other things that puzzled you and you wanted to know about. We must go on talking. I know it's not the same as talking, or having a continuing dialogue, for me to write long monologues and then have to wait for an answer – but it's still a form of communication, especially when you haven't any other!

And I want to say again what I've always said: your questions always make me think, and because you want serious answers, I'm the person who learns most. So, whenever you ask me anything it benefits all of us: not only does it satisfy your curiosity, but enriches me as well, and among us we all really learn how to think. What little I know I have always learnt in that sort of way – by necessity, when ordinary, candid people ask genuine questions because they *want to know* the answers. That's the best way to get the truth, and get deeper into it. It's a very good thing to go through the world asking questions about what's happening around you – and never being afraid to ask questions even if you're afraid they'll sound silly. Only the foolish, the conceited, and people who don't know anything, think they know it all already. If ever you meet anyone who's 'been around a long time', steer clear of them. People who've 'been around' like that tend to be people who've never been anywhere. If you want to start to learn about anything, the first thing is the need to know – simple curiosity; and curiosity always has something ingenuous and fresh about it – which people who haven't got it don't understand. In every adult worth anything there's always a sort of child inside – which means a fantastic delight in learning things, and a great generosity in passing them on. Never be afraid to ask questions! And, as I've always told you, everything, but *everything*, can be explained to a child. Indeed the best foundation for any future adult is to have had people around him as a child who worked on that assumption. Children are serious people, and must always be taken seriously. But, of course, as I write this, I suddenly realize that of my children, only one is still a child – my little Mafalda in blue jeans – and the other two are two great full-grown layabouts! But that doesn't stop our being good friends, I hope – in fact we can start talking better than ever.

I'm afraid I'm lecturing you rather a lot ... The trouble is that I've nothing to read today – they haven't any books here, and that's death as far as I'm concerned. And they won't let my fellow-prisoners pass me on any from their library. I really haven't much to do – I go on taking my walks round this tiny room. At first it made me a bit dizzy going round and round in such a small space, but I've got used to it now – it's amazing what you can get used to! – and I do it regularly. And I've changed the way I work out the distance. Remember how I said that 150 paces were about equal to 100 metres? Well, having to count was a nuisance, and became a bit of an obsession, so I've now worked it out by timing, instead. I take sixty steps a minute (that's very slow – I don't rush it), which is the equivalent of 36 metres; that means I do approximately one kilometre per half-hour. I look at my watch, and start walking; when I've walked for half an hour or more, then I know how much exercise I've taken. Doing it this way, I can think while I'm walking. It's surprising the things I think of. I know this sounds dotty ... But when you're in a situation like this, you have to try every possible expedient to keep yourself going. You must never give up. I've been thinking a lot lately about a superb book I read ages ago by a doctor – I think he was Austrian; he was a Jewish psychologist, and spent the war in a German concentration camp. He had been near death himself, and had seen almost all his friends die, and in this book he talks about his experience: how even in the most terrible times he never gave way, but somehow kept up his morale. He used to get up, and make himself clean and tidy, and prepare to spend each day as well as possible, and so on. And it was really the *will* to keep going that kept him going ... I read that book over twenty-five years ago, when I was doing psychology, but the memory of it keeps coming back.

My darlings, I expect that by the time you actually get all these notes Alfonso will be home, and you can read them together – which is why I want to tell you now how enormously I admire his plays, especially the unpublished work that no one has read yet; most of all for the last one, *El camarada oscuro*. But I had never really understood what he meant about multi-level tragedy; I accepted it in theory, but I didn't really *feel* it – and indeed I told him so. In certain scenes in those last plays there was something that surprised me – unpleasantly – and puzzled me. Now, after the experience I've been through, and as I go on reflecting about it here, in my cell, I can see clearly what a tremendous discovery it is – for the theatre and for literature in general – this concept of his in which the whole range of tragedy and comedy forms a synthesis that hasn't as yet been analysed (and is therefore still a bit startling). As far as I know, no one has written about it before. Yet surely it is that richness and complexity that is what 'realism' is all about. (I won't go on about it, because he understands what I mean – we've talked about the subject together so often.) The deepest, most agonizing, knife-thrust wounds, the moments of supreme tragedy, these are combined with absurd experiences or comical situations that have their own kind of grandeur. Reality must always be like that – and anything else, however worthy it may be, is *inevitably* a distortion. It is sobering to think that, not till I came *here*, and had such appalling experiences, did I think deeply about it and really understand in depth what he means by the multi-level tragedy that obsesses him so. But I'm convinced that one day people will study it as one of the greatest discoveries of literature! All I can do is say over and over, for Alfonso, that favourite cliché of ours: 'The more I know you, the more I love you.' As for you, my darlings, I can only advise you to read your way slowly through all his unpublished plays . . .

I stopped there, because I had to go out and make a statement. I'm afraid now that I shan't be able to go on writing. It's dreadful to think of it, but so it appears. I can't say any more now. The slightest imprudence on my part, the slightest wrong move – and they'll take away my paper and pencil.

(*Two hours later, everything was taken away from me. This journal was returned to me weeks later by the prison Governor. It had been typed out without a break, just as I wrote it. I wanted it like that, so that one day I could make a thorough study of the state of mind I was in when I wrote it.*)

LETTERS

Yeserías
19 October 1974

Darling children,

This letter is to you all, but specially to Juan; he needs to hear most because he's so far away, and I imagine he has had only the most minimal and confused information. So, Juan darling, I'm sitting down just as I used to sit at the kitchen table last year, to tell you how much I've been thinking of you these past few weeks. In the endless hours I spent in the DGS I had more than enough time to think about the people I love, and you were one of them. But it comforted me to know that you are living a full life, studying and working, and surrounded by friends who love you. You are experiencing the kind of solidarity which one can only feel if one really *loves* human beings and understands what an immensity of energy there is within us all. Everything that has happened to me in this past month (can it really be only a month?) seems like a nightmare, though the sad fact is that I did not dream it. I know you are mature enough to realize that none of what has been said in the papers, and the other media, is true. You know me. We've talked such a lot about what's going on in the world, and you know very well what my ideals are, so you know I would never have taken part in anything that was *anti*-human – you know that what we have to fight for is for man to be able to think, and study, and become aware of the reality around him. The truth – which they've done their best to distort – will win through when the time comes, and everything will be in its right place again. But I needn't go on. Your letters have always made me so proud of you, and I know they'll make me prouder than ever from now on. Our life goes on;

we're a very close family, like so many Vietnamese families, and like those Chilean families you know from your college. We love one another, and we love our fellow human beings, and each one of us will work and study as hard as we can; in this respect, age makes no difference – I still feel young and bursting with life, and ready to carry on. I'm not Yaya's daughter for nothing – poor Yaya! They had to break the news to her gradually, or she'd have died of shock! Anyway, what I want to tell you is that I'm very well – both in health and in spirits – and I've worked out a plan for my life here: a life of study, writing (I'm thinking of writing a novel) and reading. Alfonso is going to carry on with his book on the imagination – his *magnum opus*, which will really make a stir when it's published, I know! – and you must carry on too. Here's Pablo, taking charge of the house so efficiently and with such a sense of responsibility – *and* so cheerfully. And little Eva, who's growing up fast, doing her job getting top marks at school. You might say that the TIO MAROMA family are all being educated at the State's expense at the moment! – I really am overwhelmed to see how smoothly everything is going when there are such masses of difficulties and problems. Darling Juan! this is my birthday greeting (though the letter will get there a bit late), a greeting full of love, and joy and hopes for the future. During the time I was in solitary confinement here, in this prison – seventeen days altogether, I wrote a kind of journal for all of you; one day you'll get it. At least – the interrogator promised me that he'd give it to you, but you must be patient, Eva darling – oh, you were looking so lovely this morning that now I hardly know what to say to you. What good friends you are living with – give them lots of love from me, and tell them I have no words to express how grateful I am for their kindness. One day we'll all be together, and then I'll hold your hand, my love, and take you off by yourself and we'll talk about our own special things. Do you remember the times we used to spend talking, especially in bed? You made me all nice and warm – but I don't miss that now, because there's something that makes me even warmer – your eyes, looking at me through the window of the visiting room: they come right inside me – you seem to be looking straight at my heart, and your look remains.....................[*illegible*].....................my whole body. It makes me feel wonderful, Eva darling! Pablo, please do tell X— how grateful I am for the kindness she has shown us. I know that you have everything you want in her house; in fact I think you could even learn French with her girls, if they liked that idea. There's nothing adequate I can say to convey how proud I am of you – but then you've only reacted as I always knew you could. After all the years we have been friends, and talked, and really exchanged ideas, it could hardly be otherwise. When there's been the kind of shared life we have had, with such a marvellous father as yours, and with our really living in accordance with what we believe, anything else would be impossible. That alone gives me courage to face the future; people may think that I'm destroyed, I've collapsed, I've lost the will to live – but I can assure you that I feel rich and happy, and full of faith and hope in the future. I hope Alfonso will soon be out, and you can all be together again; the worst thing must be for you, Pablo, my fair-haired fleet-foot messenger, having to go from one prison to another, taking messages back and forth, *and* taking the helm of the boat in such a terrible storm – even though we know it's going to keep afloat and will come safely into port in the end. I've told you the food is fine, and there's absolutely nothing I need. If anyone ever sends me anything I'll share it with everyone else, and I'll like getting it more for the love it represents than anything else. (*That's* what really keeps one going!) Our bedrooms are comfortable – we are several to a room – but we spend most of our time in the library, the courtyard and the TV room. As you know, I am anti the consumer society and the wasteful way so many people live nowadays. In this sense I've got all the material goods I need – pencil, paper and books – and I find I can actually think better in these conditions. Tell all our friends that I am thinking of them – Teresa, Tere, Azucena, etc. etc. – and tell them they can think of me quite happily, and that I'm smiling as always. Give a big hug to Pepito and Alicia and the children. I always knew Aurora and Pepe were marvellous in-laws, so I wasn't surprised when Alfonso told me how great they'd been; tell them I love them very much. I am grieved that Grandma should have been subjected to such malicious rumours, specially since I left her so unwell and depressed. But she's very brave, and she'll soon find out the truth. Give them all much, much love – including María Aurora and precious little Raquelín. This letter was mainly for Juan, and I'll end by coming back to him. Darling, I hope this letter will reassure you. An old peasant in Manzanillo once said this to me: 'A man is really great when he shows what is in him.' It's true. Man is full of possibilities and riches; and it all has to be channelled and focused and directed to the future in a progressive opening outwards. I've learnt a great lesson from simple people – the people on the farm where I wrote my book, the Vietnamese woman who talked to me that day about her life in Paris, and the men I met in our own village. Nothing that happens to us is ever just forgotten. No experience is ever lost – it's all so much energy that is stored up. As human beings who have the intelligence, our duty is to study, and investigate things, and keep on learning all the time. I'm so happy that you're with friends for your eighteenth birthday: you're a millionaire in your capacity for learning and questioning things, and I think that's the best inheritance we can leave you! Hurry off to see them all – Melba, Anisia and Pepe, Cuco and Alba, and all of them. Tell them I love them, and that I'm smiling as I say it; tell them there's nothing in my life that conflicts with what I feel and think, and that one day, when all this legal business come out into the open, it will all be clear, and I shall be happy! Happy birthday, my darling Juan,

EVA

My darlings,

Your visit this morning left me feeling so happy, and strong enough to face another week, as did the news that there'd been a letter from Juan, and that he sent me so much love. Seeing you and hearing from him, so far away, gave me the lovely feeling that all his warmth, and emotion and love were really close to me – they seem inside me and all around me, in my heart and in my mind, as I think of you all. You, and of course Alfonso, are my closest friends, and that in itself gives me a reason for carrying on. I feel a bit panicky when I think how many things I want to say to you, and how little room I have to say them in. Shall I begin with Eva? Do you realise you're more of a little Mafalda than ever? I've talked about you such a lot to the other prisoners, with the result that you're going to get a really *lovely* necklace: it's a present from a sweet girl of twenty, and she made it out of breadcrumbs, which she dried and painted. That little purse was made so lovingly, and the other one, which I'll give you next time, was also made by a young girl – twenty-one. These little gifts from prison are truly priceless, because of the love that goes into the making. Tell Camelia and Teresita that if they'd like little purses, I'll make them for them too. And, darling, you must always tell me about your problems, won't you? If ever you can't, you must talk them over with Pablo; he's already someone you can lean on, and I'm absolutely sure he'll have better solutions to suggest than any grown-up you talk to – he knows you so well, and he has such a sense of humour, and he really does love you. Not everyone is lucky enough to have the kind of brothers you've got – and remember that when you ask questions, when you ask for advice, you're not the only one who's learning something – the people who have to answer you also learn a lot. In fact we really do each other a favour by asking each other questions. And I hope you also realize that needing to ask questions, needing to be curious to know about things, is one of our deepest human needs; it's that that makes one look into things, collect facts and examples, and then be able to make comparisons; in other words that's how one's mind develops, and that, combined with sensitivity of feeling, is what the humanity of human beings is based on. So, asking questions is always a good thing and very necessary – especially for a child; in fact it can be a very bad thing *not* to ask, because it leaves you with all kinds of doubts and fears, and you go on feeling insecure, and your insecurity then increases when you come to realize how little you know about life – and then you get more and more frightened, and a whole series of problems builds up, which can end up by actually making you ill. Whenever there's something you want to know, you must always *ask*, and when you have problems you must always talk about them. I know that when you want to ask questions there may not always be someone kind and sensible around to go to, but as a rule, the more intelligent and sensitive a person is, the more they'll listen, and the more prepared they'll be to take the trouble to give you a satisfactory answer and help to solve your problems.

It's only foolish people full of pride and vanity who won't listen, and that's why it's sometimes said that the wise are like little children. Well, perhaps I'm going on too long about this . . . Anyway, let's just say : Never stop asking questions – Pablo, Alfonso and Juan will all help you a lot, and I'll try to learn along with you and hope to teach you something as well. When people who love one another also understand one another, then no difficulties from outside can really hurt them, or be too much to bear. One day I'll tell you what I think a family ought to be like – we have talked about it a bit before : certainly not like so many of our friends' families, conventional and only united on the surface – nor should it be abolished, as some people suggest who really don't know what they're talking about. We believe in a new kind of person, and we believe in a new sense of family; and it would be strange if that didn't lead us to act in a different way as a result. Have I said enough? Today I'm being the mother who gives good advice – so I must ask you, Pablo, about your adventures – your walks around the back streets of Madrid. You're so sensible to do that. With your love of literature I can just see you observing things, and trying to find out all you can about what goes on in that unknown world dotted around the city ... I did the same at your age, and I was full of plans to put the people I met into books. Your father didn't............[*illegible*]

....

I hardly know what to say to Juan : what can I say, darling? That I'd like actually to *see* your letter? Could you write me letters that they can send on to me? I'd like to have a recent photo. Everything I've said so far is to you as well. I'll just add that on the 29th you'll have your glorious eighteenth birthday, and I'm so happy that you're with good friends. I'll drink your health – in milky coffee – what else? ... I've got a few jobs for you. First : Pablo, could you go and see Angelina and Eduardo. My thoughts are continually with them – more than they suspect. They were with them from the time I was arrested, and I felt miserable when I thought about young Eduardo. I used to talk such a lot with Angelina on the subject of children, and she is so sensitive, and so concerned about them, that I can understand what she is going through now. Tell her that I'm with them in spirit, that they mustn't feel too bad; tell her Eduardo is a great boy, a great man; he's a serious, responsible boy, and I know he'll manage to come out of this all right. Sometimes misfortunes turn out to be blessings, and open up new perspectives. What can I say to them? Give them my love – I love them all. What else can I say? I'm sure the truth *will* out. None of the news you hear is true, it's all just newspaper sensationalism. Don't be downhearted, my dears! Give my best love to Carmen too, and thank her so much for all her kindness and all the trouble she's taken – more than *anyone*. I'm so grateful that she's sending books to Alfonso, and all the other things. I've no idea what it's like at Carabanchel; I think it may be a bit cold, and if he isn't with anyone else there'll be no one to lend him any clothes or anything ... But then I know you will have thought of everything. And many, many thanks for the parcel and everything you sent me! I'm really well fitted out now! ... There are still a few little things I need, and I've written them on a piece of paper which I enclose. I know that our friends – true friends indeed! – are looking after you all as well as you could possibly be looked after; please give them all my thanks. Thank you, thank you. Now – back to Juan: I wish you would send me a long letter (several kilometres!) telling me all about your life this year, your plans for the second year, your work, your worries and your love life. Do you realize that I spent *hours* – a whole afternoon – describing the system of education over there to the interrogator? It's even more important now than it was last year for us to write very often. Funny things, too. What's going to happen to our sense of humour? I know you realize how important humour is if one is to have a realistic and all-round view of life. Only people who feel passionately can really laugh properly – without fear and without bitterness. Because for them laughter is a liberation. And only people who can be merry can then think about really sad things, and view them critically, and take an objective attitude and see them with a sense of humour. You must get a move on – you've got a whole world to explore and conquer! Oh dear, I'm coming to the end of this paper, and I'm afraid I'll have something else to say that there won't be room for. Yesterday I got a letter from Bandrés, the lawyer. Apparently one can only designate one defending lawyer for the Military Tribunal, and I've now designated him; can you let M— and Papa know? (That doesn't mean that Bandrés can't *consult* other lawyers.) About Yaya – it's very important to find out whether she got my long letter, because it will have done a lot to set her mind at rest. If she didn't get it, you must ask for it – it's terribly important to make sure letters get through, and if they don't M— must do something. They've been withholding letters for forty days now, with appalling consequences. Eva: I really laughed when I thought of what you said about all your friends' fathers planning to learn German so that you can understand them when they talk French! Oh, how I long to see you! Do tell me when you write what sort of room you are sleeping in, and where you're studying, and everything. Much *much* love to the whole family: Anisia, Pepe, Pepito, give them all kisses from me. Tweak Grandma's ear and tell her to look after herself. I must stop. It's Sunday, a sunny Sunday, and there's peace for a little while, because everyone has gone to see some awful film or other. They'll soon be back and my peace will be over; but I'm now sitting like a lizard in the warm sun, thinking and dreaming of you, in a corner of the courtyard. Some day we'll all lie out like this together some-where in the mountains. I love you so much, so *infinitely* . . .

EVA

Darling children,

I saw two of you yesterday (I always feel the absence of
Juan, – I miss his athletic figure and his smile), and as I write
this, I realize that very possibly I'll only see one of you next
Saturday. So be it. It's all for your good, and everyone else's
too, because for that very reason – knowing that you're studying, that your minds are at rest, and that you can think clearly
undisturbed by black clouds – Alfonso and I feel a sense of
peace which will help us a lot in the midst of all this unexpected disaster. I do hope all goes well, Pablo darling! and
give my special love to María Luisa – don't forget! – and tell
her that it comes not only as from a friend, but with all that I
feel as a mother for you as well. Good luck, my love. I did
say a while ago that we are now a state-supported family,
didn't I? I won't go on giving you advice (as I did to poor
Juan – he must almost have drowned in it!). Get all the education you can, and then you can tell us about everything when
you come back – which I hope will be soon, more especially
as I think you can only come when Alfonso has been released.
But I won't say any more about that now. Juan: Milagros
didn't tell us a great deal about you – or at least if so not much
has come to me – but one thing really gave me pleasure: she
said you took the news of all that's happened here like a real
Vietnamese! Who could ask for more? Thank you very much,
Juan darling, for that message! But do please write a bit more.
Of course, as I think of it, this whole business of letters is becoming a kind of extraordinary game of combinations and
changes: my letters to you, which you have of course (who?)

to photocopy twice over, one copy for Juan and one for Pablo. And the same with Alfonso's letters when you get them. Then your letters when they come, which have to be copied, one copy for Alfonso and one for me, and the original to be kept by you (Eva?) to read to the family. When you think about it, we could really do with an office to handle it all! Perhaps Uncle Pepito could take charge of the whole business, because it's easiest for him. I think it would be best if you could come with someone older next Saturday, Eva (Pepe, Pepito or Aurora?) so that we can arrange all this, and various other things. Pablo: you say in your letter (though Eva hasn't said anything) that you found me less cheerful than I was; it may be that I was a bit worried last week, because of not having seen a lawyer for forty-five days. But I'm happy today: Bandrés has been to see me, and given me a lot of help. He's a really warm human being, and very understanding – he inspires me with real confidence. I'm pleased with my choice, and I'd like you to tell Alfonso so if you see him before I can write. From now on I'll be able to have a bit more control over what's happening around me, and I hope I'll end up by understanding a bit more about this two months' nightmare. Eva seemed very happy and very beautiful, and I can only say (I'm sorry to keep repeating myself) that we can never repay the S—s for all they've done for her. The photos are delightful. I still haven't decided what to do with them – whether to keep them in my bag, which I always have with me, or whether to put them on the wall by my bed. I hope you'll bring me the rest, and then I'll work something out. Now I'm going to tell you about a dream I had early on Friday morning, and which – since finding out about Pablo's trip – seems almost like a premonition ... It was somewhere in Scandinavia, I'm not sure which country. Eva, Pablo and I were sitting on a great wide beach. It was cloudy, but it wasn't cold, and the sea was calm. Eva and I were very close together, looking up at the sky and all the seagulls flying endlessly round. We watched them closely, and observed their behaviour – how they flew, how they chased one another, how they criss-crossed. Suddenly we saw three of them lining up, beak to tail, forming a kind of long harpoon, and attacking a huge fish that was sticking up out of the sea. We were amazed at the intelligence this kind of combined action indicated, and Eva and I began calling Alfonso to come and see. But Alfonso couldn't come, and missed it. At that point Pablo, who was a little way off, was playing with some other seagulls, and from time to time hung on to the tail of one and got lifted up a little bit by it. Time passed and suddenly we looked and saw him with his arms spread out and each hand holding on to the tail of a group of three gulls; then another three came along close to his face, and he grasped the tail of this new group in his teeth, and thus, looking like a kind of large comet, we saw him gently borne upwards by nine birds. Slowly he rose and fell, and from time to time landed gently on the ground. He's another Leonardo da Vinci, I thought ... Then I woke up. Doesn't that seem like a premonition? A flight to Renaissance Italy? Eva: you always have such lovely dreams – why do you never write to me about them? Do keep writing, it makes me so happy. Why don't you write more, Eva darling?

There are several very young, very uneducated girls here with me – I could be their mother, and I talk to them a lot and we laugh together. I've shown them photos of my sons – I show them off whenever I can! – and they say they wish the boys had been arrested instead of their mother, etc. Most of them have family problems; basically they are all very much in need of being valued and understood, and I've tried to explain certain things to them – how important it is first to develop as human beings, growing in emotion and real friendship, and love, with other people, before starting to worry about theoretical problems which they can't understand fully anyway, at their age. We talk a great deal, and sometimes when they are unhappy I'm able to comfort them a bit. One of these 'daughters' of mine is the same age as Juan. She's very intelligent but seems rather bewildered; she's got bogged down in books she can't really understand or assimilate. Giving her advice makes me long to have you with me, and I think about you more than ever. She's promised to make a sketch for you which I'll pass on. Sometimes we read aloud together, and it reminds me how we used to do that on Saturday mornings ... Don't ever stop reading! Eva: there's one book which we read aloud and enjoyed a great deal when Juan was little: *Don Quixote*. You're just about the right age for starting to read some of it. Pablo would read it to you very well – he can do it when he gets back; meanwhile, do bury yourself, as they say, in good books. I *wish* you'd write to me, Eva darling. One letter a week isn't much, and I'd be able to see how your handwriting is getting on, and how well you write and express yourself. You say nothing ever happens – but that's not true. A lot of things are always happening to everyone; it's a matter of learning to describe them, and that comes with the habit of writing. If you wrote a little bit each day, you'd see how easy it is. Why not write a journal for me, and send it to me every week? Monday would be a good day and then I'd get it on Wednesday. How about that? What about you, Juan? Tell me what you're reading, and what you're doing: I'm terribly interested in everything that concerns you. Pablo: you'll have to start writing proper letters – I must get news of you every week! Before I forget, let me say thankyou for all the things you've sent me – you and all our friends. And please, even if it can only be by phone, give my fondest love to Eduardo's parents. Where is he? What's happening to him? Has he got a good lawyer? I can get him one of the ones that come here. I keep hoping that Alfonso is with him, but I don't know a thing. When you come on Saturday – whoever comes – can you bring me a refill for my ballpoint – the one you brought is no good, it's a Parker and I asked you for a fine-point 'Inoxcrom 55'. This is *very* important, because I spend all day writing, and without it I shall come to a standstill. I write more than I read. So many things have happened just lately – I feel as if I could burst, and all I can do is write! Most of my letters go to Alfonso – he needs communication with the outside world in a way you don't, and I need more than ever to communicate with him. That was a marvellous sonnet he sent Juan for his birthday! It's fantastic having someone so gifted in the family! You know, Pablo, I thought you looked very thin and worried. Is there something you're not telling me? You must get it off your chest. So many problems have fallen on your shoulders lately, and it makes me anxious. You're very strong, but you must take care of yourself. Talk to friends, and when you see María Luisa, tell her everything – and cry if you need to. You must *talk* about what troubles you. I'm afraid all this has been too much for you, but don't look back : look forward – you've got a bright future, and lots of possibilities; you've got people you love around you, people whose lives are rich and full of achievement. Nothing else matters! It won't be long before all this is a misty memory, and we'll smile as we look back on it. We're going through the worst part now – but the truth will come out and we shall win in the end. That's our strength – the knowledge that we are in the right. Bon voyage, Pablo! Goodbye Eva; goodbye Juan. (Pablo, send me a telegram as soon as you are with María Luisa. For anything that concerns me it's important for you to have my lawyer's address : Juan María Bandrés, ... Any press-cuttings etc. should be sent both to M— and to Bandrés, but it's he who is my official lawyer. Write to him when you get there, and tell him your address.) The gods go with you, comrade Pablo!

EVA

Darling children,

I'm devoting Sunday afternoon to you, as I have been doing these past few weeks – a peaceful prison afternoon. It's filled with silence, because a lot of people have gone to see a film, and for me it's filled with memories and with all my love for you. There are such lots of things to say! I'll begin with Juan, because though in my heart he's here with the rest of you, he is the furthest away and it's so long since I've seen him. Oh Juan, it's such ages since I saw or heard from you! Why don't I get even a line in your own handwriting? They've only told me (and that's quite something) that you're behaving like a Vietnamese; that makes me very proud, but it worries me a bit too. I long to see your nice bold writing, and that natural way you have of expressing yourself; I want to *feel* the vitality you put into all your work and your studying. I don't even know whether my letters are getting to you. You must get your friends to manage it somehow – I *know* it's not your fault; I'm sure that there's some official interference stopping your letters getting through. Explain to them that in my situation I *need* to have this minimum contact – in fact *we need* it, because Alfonso is in just the same boat, dying just to handle a piece of paper with your writing on it. I keep wondering about your work, your reading, all your concerns; I wonder how the news of what's happening to us reached you. I've got an endless series of questions. Please try and write, Juan darling! I'm sorry to go on about it, but you mean so much to me just now, when so much is happening, so much to worry about, so many totally unexpected things ... (I want here to beg Carmen A—

to see Gustavo and pass on to him my longing to hear from Juan direct.) And now, you, Pablo: I got your splendid letter, and I'm so proud of you. I read it with my friends here. I absolutely agree with you – you're not running away, but trying to see and think more clearly. You can't imagine how much it means in the superficial world we live in to find a boy of your age saying something so profound! It's no more than I'd have expected, but it's fantastic when it happens, all the same. I take it you had a good journey, and are comfortably settled in with the d'A—s. I'll hope for more news soon. You realize I spent the whole night thinking about your journey, and whether it all went well, and whether there were any last-minute problems? Then I had a very soothing dream – one of those bird dreams I've had such a lot of lately – and it makes me happy to know you are so close to me, and yet so safe from danger. You'll have to work out a programme of studies to follow out there. It doesn't matter about the University; you're very young and your life is ahead of you, and I think you'll appreciate Rome and all its glories much more. Anyhow, I'm sure María Luisa – who I hope you'll pass on all my letters to – will be able to show you how to make the most of your time there. I'm sure that if I'd had the luck to go to Rome at your age, I'd have spent my time just wandering through the streets. Do whatever you feel is most important for you now – you know I trust you absolutely! Now, Eva: today's letter is most of all for her, because I think at her age one needs conversation more than at any other time. Do you agree, Mafaldita? One thing has been exercising my mind a lot in the past few days – I feel that there's something worrying you. Of course there must be more than one – it would be absurd to suppose that after all we've been through you could just go happily on as though nothing had happened. That would *really* be a bad sign! In fact, it's natural that you should feel miserable at times, and then at others try to forget your worries and enjoy yourself for a bit. But I want to say again what I said in one of my last letters about how helpful it is to talk about your problems; I wish you'd write to me about them so as to bring them out into the open. I know it's hard, because you must feel that we aren't alone, and that other people will read the letters – but you really mustn't worry about that. During this time especially since I've had absolutely no privacy – I've come to realize just how important our family is: it's important, and it rests on really firm foundations of love and understanding. And that's something we can really feel proud of – because if things were different, I might have felt embarrassed to talk about things that are ambiguous and unpleasant, about emotions involving selfishness, jealousy, and all the other negative feelings we have so often been able to laugh off when we were togther. On the other hand, since our relationship is honest, we are real friends and real comrades, then we can actually feel quite pleased for other people to listen in on us – or at least not mind it. Does that make sense? I wish you could just forget about the other people. The fact that they read your letters in the family where you're staying, and other people read them afterwards, mustn't make you stop writing them. Anyway – all this great preamble is leading up to the thing I'm worrying about. María Paz B— – who is a very nervous woman and finds it very hard to restrain her impulses, and who has suffered terribly in her life – threw herself weeping into my arms the other day, and told me how sorry she was for having been horrid to you in her house shortly after I was arrested. She told me how you had cried, and she'd lost her temper and hit you. Poor little Mafalda! And you've been to see me every Saturday, always happy and smiling so cheerfully, and never said a word about it! I know you well enough to know how horrible it must have been for you (as she described it) – but it'll be all right if you can think about it now, and talk to me about it, and don't keep it bottled up inside you. She's a bit rough in her ways anyhow, and a bit sick, and she's not used to children – so she thinks children don't take things in. If you can understand all that about her, then it won't worry you any more. I hope not, anyway. Though you're so young, you showed that you were the one who was grown-up and could behave like a mature person; that's quite something. But it made me sad to realize that you didn't want to upset me and so didn't tell me about it – because though the incident itself wasn't very important, anything becomes important if you bottle it up inside you. It isn't a good idea to try to forget things: you've got to be brave, and if you're worried about something, however painful it is, you must think about it, and talk it over with someone who can help, and can perhaps explain it to you. Eva darling, you must *think* about *everything, always*. I wish you'd write to me. And I don't understand why they haven't sent me the pictures you've done for me ... Anyhow, we talk on Saturdays, and we'll go on talking, and in the end we'll solve our problems. Tell me what books you're reading. Alfonso has written some really lovely lyrics for you, and some poems for Yaya and Grandma. When a letter comes from him it always feels like Christmas! My own situation remains just the same. We don't really know what's happening, or how long it's going to go on, and we all find different ways of fighting off our depression. I work quite a lot. A typical day here is something like this: I get up at 7.30 (I'm the first one – as you know I always was an early bird), and have a shower, and then read till they come to count us (to make sure we're all here and no one has escaped); then an excellent breakfast, and then I read again. (I'm trying to move from novels to essays, but it's hard to concentrate.) This stint of reading I do in the sun, in the little inner courtyard (and I'm getting very tanned). After lunch, I read a section of *Capital* with a group of girls (they're politically very naïve); and then I settle down to write. Writing is the thing I enjoy most: I go on for page after page without a break, and I think my correspondence with Alfonso – two letters per week – is very helpful to us both. At night I share a bedroom with three friends: Lieta, Carmen and Pata. That's when all the tension is released, and one can really relax. We spend most of our time laughing – we start off from some piece of nonsense, and one silly remark leads to another until we end up talking a kind of whole surrealist language. It would be really hard to survive all that they're doing to us if we couldn't laugh! At eleven or so, we put out the light and go to sleep ... And odd though it seems, I usually have the most lovely dreams; but you mustn't think that means that when I wake up and have to face reality again it makes me sad. In spite of all the misfortune and suffering and harassment, there's one thing that is still more important: the fact of your lives – *so* rich and *so* full of possibilities – of your future, of your smiling faces (I always picture you all smiling, all of you, Juan, Pablo and Eva), and the way you all look so alert, so direct, so full of curiosity, so bursting with intelligence ... How lucky I am to have children like you and a husband like Alfonso! I feel he is always watching over us and protecting us, and showing us by his example how splendid it is to be a human being if you really are one! And then I think of all our friends, our comrades in so many places all round the world, whose hearts beat with ours, who are thinking the same thoughts and concerned with the same problems. Then, every morning, I get up again, and I look ahead: I'm making plans for studying, for self-improvement, for future work; I keep reminding myself that no experience is ever valueless, that it all remains with us, and gets saved up as a creative potential which will some day be converted into fresh energy to assist future generations. There are some things that are never lost, and indeed some things you actually gain when others are lost – like dignity, and reason. Please write to me soon! Much love to all our friends, to everyone. I love you,

EVA

p.s. Eva: say thank you very much to the S—s for their photos – their goodness to us is really fantastic. And tell them I'd like more – lots more – of Juan, of Yaya, of Alfonso, of all of you! I hope you can all sympathize with this mania of mine for photos?

My darling children,

I'm so miserly with paper that my handwriting gets smaller every day – you'll end up having to read it with a magnifying glass! Anyway. Here I am this rainy Sunday in prison in Madrid, sending out a huge hug to last for hours and hours – a hug when I can feel your hearts beating next to mine, and we seem to be clasped together so tightly that no one can separate us. Today I'll begin with my delicious Eva. Eva, it seems to me, since reading your letter, that you're becoming your old self again. I was touched by your handwriting, which was a bit wobbly (with emotion?); you'll have to keep working to improve it, but the more you practise, the better it'll get. (It's really convenient that I want a letter once a week!) As for what it said, I thought that was lovely. How true it is that 'there are so many people in the world whose minds have never developed'! I like that: it shows that you're thinking about what's going on around you, and you're paying enough attention to be critical. Well done! I *do* understand that you feel lazy sometimes, and have to make an effort to get over it and then take a run at your work. That sort of laziness is often a cover-up for depression – depression is a very sneaky thing which takes all kinds of forms, and it's a good thing if you can get rid of it and shake it off. If you keep shaking it off, it finally learns its lesson, and is too frightened to come back! Have you found that? I'm a bit concerned about your not feeling well that time in the bath, and getting cramp. Has it happened again? Cramp – if that's what it was – is when a muscle contracts and it's nothing to be frightened of, though it's certainly very painful. But you must try not to worry about things; you see, it could be just what I was talking about in my last letter – it could be some problem you're keeping to yourself, and since you're bottling it up, it's looking for an escape, and comes out in some other way! It's amazing how complicated it is being a human being, isn't it? I don't like the sound of the S—s' caretaker; she must be a very embittered woman, for some reason or other. People who are unkind to children are just showing up their own stupidity – there's so much to be learnt from children; anyway, don't worry about it – I'll send the letters to Pepito in future and that'll be all right. You must send Pacita a card; you know she's terribly fond of you, and would be sad to think you'd forgotten her, with all that's happened. I'm sure she loves you even more now; there's certainly no reason to feel ashamed about any of what's happened to us – in fact quite the opposite. Alfonso and I have always fought for a world where people can be really human – can *think*, and not just stay at the stage of the ancestral monkey! That's why we've always said that we must study, and progress, and discover how and why things happen, and not just accept what people say, and churn it out again like parrots, without really looking into things and asking questions, and so on. There's certainly nothing in all this to be ashamed of – on the contrary, we can be proud of it; and though it may look to you *now* as if everything has gone against us, it hasn't really. The papers and the radio and the TV tell the most terrible lies, and they put them out without stopping to think of the harm they're doing; but we know the truth, so none of that need trouble us – and as you see it doesn't trouble our friends either: they love us more than ever and that's because they trust us. I know, of course, that you sometimes get the feeling that everyone is looking at you, or saying nasty things about you. That's what happens when you keep a thing bottled up inside you, and don't bring it into the open – it grows and grows and you start seeing something that isn't really there. Remember how Uncle Pepito said that when

Pablo went to Miraflores, Pacita's parents gave him lots of presents? So really, you're just imagining things! Write to Pacita, and when you've made yourself do it, you'll find how wrong you were, and that she does like you. Will you do that? You've got to be brave, darling! If you overcome today's fears, you'll overcome bigger ones tomorrow! You know, even though we're apart in two prisons, Alfonso and I write to each other a lot: think of it, two letters as long as this every week! By the time you get to read them, they'll be like reading a whole novel! I was absolutely delighted to hear you are reading Chekhov – his characters are really marvellous, and later on you'll be able to read his plays. Thank you so much for your picture! It's beautiful, and I've put it on the headboard of my bed – it's like having a window open on to some magical world. I can't wait for the next one. We really are close, aren't we? Well, let's go on to Juan, my Vietnamese fighter. Did you know I got a little letter from Alba, which I found tremendously moving? It made me realize how full of love this family of ours is, and that wherever we may be, there's always this bond between us – a bond of human love and brotherhood. Now I've started waiting for letters again – when will I hear from you? I think of you out there, free, with masses of friends, full of life and activity. Perhaps even starting something new? My imagination goes no further. Milagros wasn't able to give very much information. If this gets to you – though at times I think that nothing from us will *ever* get to you – tell all our friends how much I think about them, tell them how grateful I am for all I gained from their example, and how much strength it has given me in moments of difficulty. What little I know that's worth knowing I owe to ordinary people with no intellectual pretensions, but people with real nobility who could always be depended upon. I keep thinking of all those friends on the farm! If you're ever near there, go and introduce yourself: tell them you're the son of one of those 'Spaniards'; tell them I shall always keep them in my heart, and that the book I wrote there is nothing like as important as what I learned from them – their example, the wealth of new understanding, the hope for the future. Darling Juan, when I think of you, and all the comrades – Chileans, and Latin Americans in general – who are studying with you, who know from their own bitter experience the full meaning of terror and savagery, I feel a tremendous wave of tenderness. We are one enormous family, a family spread far and wide over the world, with a single heart beating in us all. Wherever we may be, no amount of solitary confinement can separate us – we are always together: we go everywhere together, and in the end we'll all meet up. I don't know whether you've heard, but a few days ago they opened a whole new case against me relating to the death of Carrero Blanco. They're making *so many* groundless accusations against me, that I realized when it began that they chose me because they had to pick on *someone*! I'm facing this new situation with some degree of fortitude. For a long time, my logical conception of human life and of history has proved to me quite clearly the meaning of the experience we're going through here and now – nothing that happens seems strange any more – it may be painful, but it's not surprising; as Martí said: 'I have lived inside the monster ... and I know it through and through.' I want you to know that I'm fine; I'm with friends who love me – most of them girls young enough to be my daughters. Your letters are fantastic (I'm sure that you've sent me a few too, Juan, even though I've never received them), and I can only say again – and especially to you, Juan, because you're the one I haven't seen for so long – that I'm simply eaten up with pride at having such fantastic children! On the headboard of my bed I've got a lovely landscape, a picture full of light and colour – and so much love – by our darling Eva. I have the great pleasure of corresponding twice a week with Alfonso – he's such a real comrade to us all, and it's his example and honesty that have helped us all so much to think and behave like real human beings all the time. I feel extraordinarily *close* to all the people I love! I have comrades in five continents, and in the most far-off places – yet I feel their support as near me as though we could really clasp hands – perhaps because I *know* that they're in complete sympathy with me at this moment. What a difference that makes! I've just had a very personal letter from Pablo, and I'm going to answer it privately.[1] It's a lovely letter, very strong, and makes me feel very proud; in it he gives a most impressively lucid answer to a very complex problem which he was presented with by someone very cultivated, but with a rather hidebound attitude to life. His reply is sound and logical, and shows what a lot of *thought* he has given the matter — I find it a great comfort to feel I can say 'Pablo is ready to go out into the world and stand up for himself' (just as I feel Juan is). So the only one I'm still concerned about is our little Mafalda; always so cheerful, so intelligent and lively, and with such a longing to learn and to know about things — but she *is* only twelve. Will she be able to carry on the way she has been going? You must all look after her. Pablo: if it's at all possible, it would be good if you could spend a fortnight with *her* this Christmas: if you could be together for a bit, and talk things over, and read your stories to her ... I'm sure María Luisa would agree to that. But I don't want you to be the one who comes here: *you mustn't come now — that's very important.* Eva darling, on Saturday you told me that you'd been to the Prado the day before, and that you loved Goya. He's one of my favourite painters too: his power, his critical ability, his sensitivity, his elegance, the way he can pass from one thing to another and what he does is always *right* — he really was a genius. (If that word means anything any more!) I think if you were in Rome you'd see a lot of beautiful things — though seeing Pablo would be the best of all. Wouldn't that be lovely? Keep thinking about it, and talk to your uncles about the possibility. It seems to me that you really *need* to see him. Do you remember how you used to sit together on your bed and laugh like a couple of lunatics, reading *El Buscón,* or some of the stories he'd written himself, specially for you, I think? I'd be pleased if you'd do some more pictures; and *please*, write me nice long letters. And don't any of you ever forget Yaya! Keep writing to her! Pablo, don't you do any painting now? I remember when you went through that great creative fever in your Picasso period,

---

1. See pp. 187–91 for Eva Forest's reply to Pablo.

and filled the house with those amazing paintings. What about you, Juan? Do you still do any painting? I think you have a lot of talent for art, and I'm afraid you've never really developed it properly. You did such superb horses! Don't give it up – there are a lot of things you mustn't give up – especially reading! And this advice goes for all of you in fact – but specially for Juan: study as much as you possibly can, keep asking questions and finding things out – never, *never* stop being curious about what makes everything tick. How goes the history? Carmen can send you whatever books you need. I'm not reading a lot at the moment, because it's so hard to concentrate. On the other hand, I'm still reading *Capital* as my bedside book – all my library lacks now is *Don Quixote*! I feel a great sense of fellowship with Karl Marx – he's so ironic, so logical, so many-sided. I wish you'd talk sometimes about the films you see, and the plays – and things in general. Did you go to the country in the end, Eva? I've suddenly remembered the dog – she's a real hunting dog and I was so glad to hear that she's in a house where they look after her properly and take her out shooting. That's the ideal solution. All my friends here who know you send you lots of love and kisses, and María Paz hopes that one day her visitors will coincide with you, so she can see you! The other girls who don't know you send their love too, or rather they send love *to you all* – because several of them have seen the photos of the boys, and say they are going to try to get to meet you when they get out!! Well, my darlings, good-bye till next week, and all my love,

EVA

My darlings,

I've put off writing as long as possible, in the hope of hearing something from Juan (I can't feel happy at getting no news at all about you, Juan!) or an answer from Pablo (though it's too soon to expect one, really). In fact it's now very late; they collect the letters at 9.30, so I must get a move on. As usual, I'll begin with my little Mafalda – and I've got some absolutely marvellous news to give you: the Governor of the prison has given me permission to have you spend a day with me. It's to be the 8th of December, which I think is a Sunday, and I'll tell you the Saturday before what you have to do. I think they'll put us somewhere we can see each other comfortably and enjoy ourselves; and we may even coincide with Antonia's daughters, who are coming to see her too. Isn't that wonderful? I'm so happy I don't know what to do, and I'm thinking about all the presents I've got for you, what we call 'prison gifts' – i.e., things that aren't much in themselves but mean a lot. I wish you could see how nice your picture of the skiers looks stuck up by my bed. I've also put up the photos of Pablo and you (I *wish* I had some of Juan and Alfonso!), and the whole corner looks very cheerful. I love your letter with the two little red hearts at the end ... I keep looking at it and looking at it, and thinking that we'll soon see each other ... I'm so glad you've got a friend. Friends are quite hard to find at times like this, and when it happens it's fantastic. Friendship is a most marvellous thing, and it's something you need more than ever now. So let me congratulate you! – and hope that it turns out to be a *real* friendship, and grows deeper, and grows really strong. You go on to say that you're always together, and you also say that the other girls are jealous; the way you say it sounds as though you're rather pleased – are you? I know exactly what you mean, but I think it's much better not to have anyone feeling jealous of one – and if they do, it's not really something to feel pleased about. It's worrying, really, to think there are people who can feel such selfish, unkind things, so different from the way human beings should feel about each other. There – that's enough of that sermon! ... Have you written to Pacita yet? Have you finished reading the Chekhov? It would be a good thing to start on Baroja now, since you're studying him – isn't that what you said when you came last time? The school journey sounds fine, and I'm glad to see you're becoming a real traveller (like mother, like daughter!) not too concerned with comfort: third-class train fare, and small hotel ... Well done – keep up the good work! When you see Isabel, do remember to pass on my condolences over her brother's death. And give a big hug to Josefina – and all the teachers who still care about me. How is 'The Journal of Eva Sastre' getting on? I'm longing to read it. I'm writing a little journal too, which I'll show you all some day. Pablo darling, I presume by now that you've got my letter, in fact both letters: the one to everyone, and the one I sent just to you in answer to your question. I can't tell you how I miss it when you don't write – I don't mean in a sentimental sense, but intellectually, I *need* to discuss and think with you. If you only knew how much it helps me! And I'm not only talking about what's happening now, but about my situation as it has always been. Meanwhile, while waiting for the longed-for letter, I'll tell you all (Oh Juan, how I long to hear news of you!) something about what my life is like in this extraordinary place I've landed up in. We're supposed to get up at 7.30, though they don't really worry about us till they count us (they count us several times a day here to make sure we haven't gone missing) at about 8.30. Anyhow, when the bell goes, I've usually been up quite a while, sitting on my bed reading – like I used to at home. (I seem to be calmer and able to read quite a bit better now, and concentrate more, though it's still not easy.) At

8.30 we go down to breakfast (there's *always* plenty of coffee!) and they don't count us again till 9.30. We spend that time tidying up our bedrooms and other parts of the building. Then a lot of us settle down to work, or read, etc. ... this time is free, and I usually use it to write something. (From now on I'm really going to be able to get down to some sort of literary work, because they've allowed me to have a typewriter. Though in the rather unsteady state of mind I'm in – due to the uncertainty of our situation – I don't know whether I'll find myself able to concentrate.) At around 1.15, the bell goes for lunch, and they count us for the third time. The dining room is big, and the food is quite good, and quite a lot of the women are brought in things from outside, so there is a kind of food-barter system – a bit like one of those back-street bars in old Madrid! Of course there are days when very few people come, and there are others when we get cakes and all sorts of presents ... Anyway, the mood is usually pretty cheerful. At 3.30 we go up to our rooms for a siesta, though a group of women and I spend the time reading *Capital* (what lessons in method and wisdom one gets from dear old Marx!). At 4.30 we come down again (none of this timing is very rigid – it's quite flexible) and again we can read, study, chat, etc. ... This is my time for starting to get into a state, looking out for letters – when there are any! (which is why it's so important that you all send me things – friends too – even if only postcards, so I can get as much mail as possible!). At 7.30, the bell goes for supper, and after that we're free till 9.30. I usually spend this time – it's about an hour and a half – in a little inner courtyard. There's always someone else who wants to stretch her legs, and we walk several kilometres together, back and forth, till it's time to go up to our bedroom. There they count us for the last time, and lock us in; and we can then do whatever we feel like, which is generally to chat for a while, and then go to sleep. As you see, it's a pretty monastic life, and terribly monotonous. I don't think I could bear it for long if I didn't have a programme of work. That seems absolutely essential: to organize and plan one's time so as not to lose oneself in the nothingness of it all. Now of course, before my case is heard –

especially as it is so complicated – any kind of concentration is going to be very difficult ... Pablo, I wish you'd tell me what kind of things you're doing. I know you must be going to the theatre a lot (lucky you) but I'd like to know whether you're carrying on with the languages you'd started – it'd be a pity if you lost them. I imagine you've met lots of friends, and that some will become friends of all of us, and I'm sure they'll be concerned about us and our legal problems. Give them all my love. María Luisa and all her family must know that I love them like brothers and sisters ... I'm afraid I have been so bold as to form a plan for Eva to spend a fortnight's holiday with you – and them – Is that possible? It would be from about the 19 or 20 December to the 8 January. We would put her on a plane here, and you would meet her in Rome. I think she really *needs* her relationship with you – you've always been so close in the past, and it would do a lot for her to see you. Can you let me know about this? And now, Juan darling, once again, I can't express how deeply and fundamentally I miss getting letters from you – I want to see your handwriting, and your ideas. I know it's not your fault, Juan darling; there must be something (some over-zealous official?) stopping your letters getting through to us. But why? I simply don't understand it. I keep thinking about your work, about your splendid course – half work, half study – which I keep telling everyone about. I see you as a model student, and a real friend to the other kids whose parents are also far away. I know you haven't forgotten us; I know we're all close to your heart, but I really *long* to hear your voice if only on a scrap of paper ... I know you haven't turned your back on what's happened, I know you're watching, and anxiously following everything that goes on; I know you're with us in our cells, just as we're with you and all our other comrades all over the world who cherish freedom. But please, you must manage to get in touch somehow. I *need* to know that my letters are reaching you. (This is the sixth collective letter *I've* written, to say nothing of those you've had from Alfonso and Pablo.) I entrust my beloved Carmen with the delicate mission of finding out just *what* is happening. If this letter ever gets to you, give a great deal of love to our friends: Anisia, Pepe, Melba, etc. ... I'm waiting, and I'll wait as long as I have to, but I really do want some first-hand news! I must stop, because it's 9.25 a.m. on the 27th of November, and they're going to collect the letters. Though I'm concluding this letter, I feel as if I haven't said anything this time – that I've been too upset, and that we haven't really talked about the things that matter most. But what are they? There are such different sorts of days! I've just remembered quite a funny dream I had yesterday, but there isn't room to tell it here. Be sure to write to Alfonso, and *above all*, to send me photocopies of all your letters, and his; there's no problem about their being given to me. I'm finishing this letter with my folder resting on my knees. Lieta is scrubbing the floor of the little room we've fixed up as a kind of study (with tables and books, and a rule of silence); she asks me to send her love to you all – and so do Carmen, Pata, Lidia and Reme. We think of you all here – all the children of all of us – and we're anxious about how you're getting on. We're a funny lot of mothers! ... There goes the bell. Grandma darling, dear, darling Grandma, how did you find your famous son? We are thinking of you here with so much love ... We love you all – Aurora, Pepe, Aurorita, Raquelín; Pepe and Alicia and the two children – all well, I hope? – and Anita and all the family ... all of you, everyone I haven't mentioned too. (Your aunt – what must she think of me?!) Much, much love,

EVA

Pepito, did you get the telegram? You'd better buy the machine, as ours have been seized. But buy it from a shop rather than the makers, because it takes much longer if you go to them direct. I know because I've done it. (Two weeks to a month!)

My dear children,

December already! It's really odd the way time passes in here. Sometimes it seems like only yesterday that I was with you at home, and they came to search the house – do you remember, Eva? You'd just come home from your first day of school, ever so happy, to have lunch with us and to tell us about all the changes this year, and you stopped dead in the doorway ... And you, Pablo, you were in a bit of a hurry, because the University entrance exam was at four. It seems so *recent*: I can still feel how warm and sunny it was that afternoon when they took me down to the street, and we all cheerfully said, 'See you later' ... And that was almost three months ago ... On the other hand, there are times when I feel as if I'd been here a hundred years. I lose all sense of time – I can't tell you whether it's long or short. When I think about it in relation to you, and the fact that we've lost our day-to-day contact, then I feel pretty bad. It's a bit the same with place; sometimes I feel as if I'm not in Madrid at all, but in some quite strange village. When I write 'Yeserías', it might be some far-away little place barely visible on the map, I hardly know where. As you see I'm plunged into a rather strange state at present ... However, in a way it makes some things easy: thinking, for instance – I'm working and thinking over some essays I've had hanging around for years. I'm as happy here with my little typewriter as a child with a new pair of shoes! I've arranged a corner for myself in the school – the school is a great big room, with a lot of little tables, and a blackboard, the whole thing very dilapidated. It's used as a way through, because it has a door out to a courtyard, but no one actually sits here much, because everyone prefers the TV room, or the dining room or the little study. So I've put two tables together, and made a little L-shaped area for myself in one corner. I've got a radiator and a window beside me, and it's all very cosy. I've always been pretty adaptable of course. Having managed to write that book on the farm in Cuba, with chickens landing on me, frogs round the foot of my bed, and all those insects, I think I could work *anywhere* ... In fact I'm doing very well, and starting to make plans. At present, I'm jotting down some memories and experiences so as to get them quite clear, and I'll tell you about it as I go on. My head's also full of some articles, which I'll try to send you, as well as part of the five-day journal I wrote (during the seventeen days I was in solitary confinement). You'll notice that my handwriting has changed – it's much smaller. I've only just got out of bed, and I realize that I've a great many things I want to say to you ... As usual, I'll begin with Eva. How are you enjoying life with your friends? I know they are all very fond of you, and that Pablo and Teresa (the grown-ups) are looking after you as well as possible; but I'd like to hear from them too, and I hope they'll tell me if they have any problems or difficulties. It's not easy living with other people, and it takes a lot of hard work and good will to learn how to do it; it can't be learnt in just a few days – which is why it's so important to choose the people you want to live with carefully, and be able to leave them if need be. I want you to think about this a bit – really think it over, and be careful not to let yourself be carried away by what is just a momentary annoyance, *or* a momentary feeling of enjoyment. How are you? Do you want to go on staying with the S—s? We'll talk about all this more on Sunday, because it's something I'm much concerned about, and I'll have to talk about it to them too. Perhaps I'll write to them now : the journal you mention – the best thing will be to get it photo-copied, and send one to Papa and one to me – I'm *longing* to have it! I read and re-read your Saturday letters ... It's very kind of you to keep saying how marvellous we are! What does being 'marvellous' really mean? Your father and I have always tried to think about everything that happens around us, and analyse it all carefully – all the problems human beings have to cope with, all the strains and struggles, the sorrows and joys, the wars and the peace, everything that comes under the heading of sociology ... and the real meaning of history, philosophy, psychology, grammar (do you think that's a strange item?), physics ... Really, though you study all these subjects separately at school, like a whole lot of isolated boxes, they're all closely interrelated – in fact ultimately they're all one. So: we've always been concerned with all this, and of course, with all of you; and we've done what has seemed best to us, though obviously one could always have done better. Is that being marvellous? If that's what *you* think we are, then I'm very happy, my darling Eva, my poppet, my merry little Mafalda ... We'll try to go on being marvellous, and if you go on being so loving and understanding, and telling us things, you'll help us to be so! Oh, how I'm going to hug you on Sunday! I'm delighted that you saw Pacita and her family – see how right I was? The best way to deal with an imaginary fear is to confront it with reality – if you fabricate terrors in your head, you find they start affecting what you do, and then you come to believe them. This is just one more proof that you have got to be brave, and discover how things really are. You investigated Miraflores, you went to see Pacita – and now it's all okay! Well done! The friend Manuela that you speak of is someone new and important in your life, isn't she? As you come to get to know each other more and more, you'll be able to talk more and more fully, and it will be great. It is marvellous to be able to talk and say things you really mean, and not just the usual chit-chat. Talking and reading (I mean serious reading) are absolutely incomparable pleasures. Your photos are up on my bed. I keep looking at them – how beautiful you all are! And what a pity I haven't got more – some of Alfonso, Juan and Yaya ... ! Why should they have destroyed them all? What harm could there possibly be in them? One day we must really talk about fear (a terrible monster once it gets a grip on you; one must start from the first taking care not to fall into its clutches!) Tell Tere that it's quite true about the Galician stew, but only when she feels in the mood – there's no hurry. I see that both your handwriting and your style are improving – one more reason to go on reading all those excellent books you talk of. I'd like you to do me a few small pictures (like those lovely ones you used to do) in different shapes – some long, some wide etc. ... because I've got some odd spaces I could fit them into. Have you got enough clothes for your trip to Rome? See what Aunt Aurora thinks, or Alicia – they'll know what you need. On Saturday we can finalize all our plans for Sunday – oh how I'm looking forward to it! ... You say how awful you sometimes feel when you think about our not being there ... Well, collect up all those awful feelings and put them in a bag, and bring them to me every Saturday, and I'll try to melt them away with my love – I should think that if we combine the warmth of Alfonso, the warmth of Pablo, the warmth of Juan, and my warmth as well, we will produce a kind of huge bonfire quite large enough to deal with them all! Don't you think so? Darling Pablo and Juan, I haven't anything much to answer of yours, because I've had no more letters (though of course I know about your adventures in Rome, and Genoa, etc., and how much María Luisa is doing for one of you). I wait impatiently for mail – though I know there are a lot of strikes in Italy, which makes it difficult. And it's hard from Cuba too, but I keep on hoping ... With you, Juan, I feel as though I'm talking in a complete vacuum – I don't ever know whether you hear what I'm saying, and therefore I don't know what to say. What happens to your long weekly letters? I'm sure there are seven or eight pages in them sometimes! Tomorrow will be Alfonso's and my nineteenth wedding anniversary. We'll have a special celebration, a special sharing of ideas and feelings, even though it's at a distance. Even now, I feel as though some extraordinary explosion had taken place in the centre of our family, and the shock waves had hurled us apart like so many bits of shrapnel, to great distances; but I don't feel at all unhappy. It seems almost like a healthy kind of expansion – painful, but honest and open – a kind of creative broadening out; we've been catapulted into space, like seeds that'll some day reproduce themselves. What is really fortunate is the way we have always been able to understand one another so well, and talk so much ... When I consider how most family problems result from 'compression' – oppression and repression – this expansion of ours seems quite extraordinary; it's like a kind of finale (or a beginning?) – like that amazing film of Vittorio de Sica's, *Miracle in Milan*, when they all fly away on broomsticks. What a liberation, eh? I think it's a great thing for each of us to be getting experience, and all different experiences. One day we'll meet and compare notes, and what a fund of richness, and happiness and freedom we'll have amassed! We must make the most of all that's happening. We must read, study, and above all live – and observe what we are living through and meditate upon it; there is no finer basis for true knowledge than what we learn through our senses. We must look, and see, and feel things, and be amazed – and not go through life like so many sleepwalkers! Pablo is really in the best possible situation to do his creative work – it's almost too good to be true! ... What a delightful family the d'A—s are – how I wish I could be with them right now in some nice bar in old Madrid! And Juan – could there *be* better experience for a future doctor than to be working in the public health service of a country in mid-transformation? And my little Mafalda – what a lot of things she's had to experience and think about! Though they're hard to bear, it's times like this that 'forge' us as human beings. 'Thus is the steel tempered' – do you remember that book? Do you remember how movingly Juan talked about it? How sorry I am now that I never read it! Lieta has woken up now – she's an early bird too. The bell will soon go. Another day. Will it be long or short? Will there be any surprises? In this limited space, and in this time – which as I said at the beginning, is so very peculiar – and in this 'ongoing process' we're involved in, life is far from monotonous; quite the reverse: uncertainty, knowing that something new may happen at any moment, anxiety, doubts, questions and all sorts of answers ...

I shall try to forget them all as I work at my typewriter, with the *utmost* discipline! (I'm sorry but my ballpoint has given out now, and I've spent an hour painfully trying to force out the letters.) Much, much love.

EVA

Darling children,

The first thing I must tell you is how terribly happy I am: it looks as though our problems – our communication problems, that is – are being resolved. Within a few days I had a visit from Eva *and* a letter from Juan – the letter I've been complaining about for so long! However, I must be systematic, and I'll begin as always with the youngest – my little Mafalda. Do you know that I felt really happy when you left me? You might think I shouldn't have, but I did ... seeing you was like getting an injection of happiness which is still working, and will go on working for a long time. So I just want to say a few small things. Your picture is lovely, and my friends are queueing up to see it; they all want one, so you'll have to set to work – but not till after you've finished your exams, of course. Hey – how did the history go? I think you knew it all pretty well; did you see the article in this week's *Triunfo* about American independence – talking about Bolívar and Sucre; if not, you could ask the S—s. How was the maths exam – okay? I'm a bit less happy about your maths, but I imagine that if there's something you don't understand you can ask one of the 'brains' in the class ... I know this is a very full week for you – but by the time you get this letter it'll be over. You know Aunt Aurora will go out with you to buy the shoes you want? One of my friends here is giving them to you as a present, so you must really get exactly the kind you like, and enjoy having them. As for the holiday, this very day Uncle Pepe is going to talk to Alfonso and we'll decide; you may decide you'd prefer to have a quiet time in Madrid, but we'll see. I must congratulate you on how good your handwriting is getting – and your spelling is perfect, which not everybody's is! ... I stopped at this point, because the post came, and, oh joy! I got a letter from Alfonso, and two from Eva with her journal. What a lot of love and tenderness there is in it! Oh darling, it's you who are marvellous! And the note telling me how much you enjoyed Sunday! I'm so delighted to hear you say that, because it was a glorious day for me, but I was afraid you might have found it a bit depressing – and now I know you didn't. That is just how it should be – one should always find out the truth, and then one knows things and does not live with delusions. You've seen what excellent conditions I have for writing, and reading and studying, and you've seen what nice friends I have, and how fond they are of me. All I *haven't* got is the physical freedom to go out as I please into the wide world – but that day will come ... If you could know how happy I am now, at this instant: with your letters and your various journals on my table, all waiting for an answer – I'm so proud to have children like you ... You say Manuela has had flu and lost her voice – how is she now? I'm already getting to like her, because I know she is your friend – perhaps I'll make her a cap: would she like one? and what colour? Did Teresita like the waistcoat? Do let me know. The Chekhov stories you've been reading must be wonderful – can't you give me some idea of the impression they make on you in general? When you write, try to tell me something of what you're feeling, and thinking – really try to express *yourself*. It's a bit hard at first, but you'll find you come to enjoy doing it bit by bit. You'll see. I'm beginning to read now, you know. Up to now it's been difficult, and I've preferred writing, but now that I've heard from Pablo – and from Juan! – and I've had a visit from you, I'm feeling a lot better. Pablo my darling, my fair, slim, agile, dreamy darling Pablo: yesterday I got your journal as well. I gather from it that you still haven't had my letter to you; it went by way of Miraflores, and I'm sorry to have delayed it in my desire to get it photocopied. (I was perhaps over-anxious in wanting Alfonso to read it too.) By now I'm sure you must have received it. Was it any help?

I need you to help me by telling me your problems, and making me feel I can help you. And I see from your journal that you're well, though rather – very much? – worried about us, naturally enough. But the general impression I get is happy, though I'm missing one letter still – or several? The fact is that this morning I've been rather worried about you, thinking you were unhappy. Uncle Pepe showed me a letter from María Luisa, who says she's concerned that you seem a bit withdrawn and don't go out much; I can't remember exactly – I shan't actually read it till I get a copy, but I gathered that she was worried about you. But I'm not sure how serious all that really is. I know you are reserved and you like being alone; you're happy if you can read and write. I do think, though, that you should make the effort to see something of Rome, to walk round and talk to people a bit. I realize that you are always more involved in things than you seem to be – I know you watch and see things, and miss nothing, even though you appear so absent-minded; so María Luisa's letter didn't really worry me too much, and I'll wait to hear more from you. But I wish you'd tell me about it. I think there are times when you *feel far away*, especially now, when you could be so useful here. I understand that (and the same goes for Juan), but the situation is such that you *must stay abroad*. That doesn't mean to say that either of you is cut off from us – on the contrary, you're kept up to date about *everything*. By knowing what happens day by day to us, you can be extremely useful in this endless case as it progresses. (Above all, the more and better you are prepared, the more useful you will be: the more you study, in the most profound sense of the word.) The beginning is always the worst. The problem of adaptation, especially when you don't know the language (and what a vital tool language is!) means that you're a bit isolated, but that you'll get over. You were asking about Eduardo. He's been let out of solitary confinement, and a few days ago he and I were subjected to a confrontation before the interrogator. He's getting better. I hear from Alfonso that his parents were pretty cheerful. It's been terribly hard – an experience they can never forget. Mari Luz is still in solitary – I think she's the only one in our case who still is. Antonio is recovering his sight – he'd become almost blind. Generally speaking, it may be said that we're all alive and thinking – the most important thing of all on occasions like this (and all other occasions, too!); for myself, I feel sure that it will all soon be cleared up, and we'll have won our fight. So don't worry: we're all in fine fettle here. Prison offers excellent opportunities for work. Alfonso has begun working on a play. I keep at it almost all day – perhaps it would be better to falter from time to time when one thinks of all that is happening to our oppressed comrades in Latin America, in Palestine, in Chile, or in Vietnam? Oh, those Vietnamese women – so exquisite and fragile-looking – how encouragingly they smiled when they said, 'We shall overcome!' I don't think I'll ever forget that – do you remember them in Versailles, Juan? They gave us such a sense of warmth and courage (and in theory we were supposed to be the ones who were encouraging them!). Please, Pablo darling, don't keep anything from me. If you change your views, if you'd prefer some different solution for the immediate future, tell us, and we'll see if it can be managed. Nothing is impossible, you know. Juan, my dearest, your letter finally got here; it's a bit more nervous and restrained (and I absolutely understand why) than your letters used to be – but it was your writing, it was your feelings, it was *you*. I'm beginning to hope that my letters are *all* getting to you and you therefore have some idea of what is happening. For you to *know everything* seems to me what matters most – both as your mother, and as one who hopes to be a revolutionary – i.e. a woman who thinks. Information is *the* basic thing; you mustn't overlook the slightest thing, and you must take account of all the facts at your disposal before making a judgement or forming an opinion. I know it's difficult when we are thousands of miles apart, and with all the mass of obstacles impeding it. But there must be no obstacles to knowledge! And if you really want to know, you'll find out, however hard it is. For instance, you must know that neither Alfonso nor I have had anything to do with the things they are accusing us of. We've devoted our lives to the struggle to help human beings be really Human –

better than people can be in most places in the world today. We want all their work to bear the imprint of freedom, and to create and develop their intelligence – but you already know what we want and how we think. And you know we shall never abandon our principles. It is this that makes us so strong, and keeps us going and keeps us united now. But I think it is vital for you to get news of what is actually happening here. To know we aren't alone. That there are a lot of people all over the world who are concerned over what's happening to us, and conveying their solidarity in one form or another – priceless, necessary solidarity. Your letter lasted me for quite a while, but now I need more! You can write to me whenever you want. I feel as though I'd lost several months of your life – that journal you sent me – or rather us – was fantastic! Could you bring it up to date? You sound incredibly busy. I realize that you're learning a great deal. Clearly medicine, as you see it and practise it, is something quite new and different. It has a lot in common with sociology ... It really is preventive medicine – with the doctor finding out about living conditions, the state of people's houses, advising, helping, talking things over ... How marvellous it would be to be able to overcome all the difficulties that arise out of simple ignorance! You'll have to develop your powers of persuasion, to try to make people understand that they mustn't just do what they always have done. The experience you're going through now will make you a real man – an all-round doctor who can be of use in whatever part of the world he finds himself, as a doctor should be. Well done! I note that you seem – still – in good spirits, which makes me very happy; I really think happiness is something that comes from an open-minded attitude to life, an attitude in which there can be tragedy, but never bitterness. The way is hard and full of obstacles, but the sky looks promising and throws light on the long journey. No one, no one going forward with such hope can fail to have the last laugh, the final victory. Your pictures (with hints of Quevedo) show a lot of creative ingenuity – don't you draw in your spare time any more? (I imagine the mention of spare time is itself something of an irony?) Do you read? What? Please, when you answer, refer to my letters – I mean my questions! Are you smoking? What about Diana? I don't know when you'll get this, but whenever it is, please ring up my friends – Melba, Pepe, and Anisia, and Cuco, and everyone, – and give them much love. By the way, do you know whether Tencha is there? If you could ask her daughter to give her my love I'd be very grateful, because I've lost her address (they took away all my addresses at the DGS), and though I *could* write to the President of Mexico, I'd rather you did it! I'm coming to the end of my paper, my darlings. This limitation of space is one of the things I mind most about being in prison – because it prevents me going on to subjects I want to chat about in a leisurely way. Anyway – if you get my letters soon, that's a lot to be grateful for ... We'll be together in another letter next week. I wonder what news you'll have? Pablo darling, don't fail to answer *by return*. Juan, please write a bit more and tell me more about what you're doing ... Another day I'll tell you something that happened to some friends of mine. And you, my darling little Mafalda, my poppet, my funny-face, take good care of yourself, because I thought you seemed a bit coldy and looked rather peaky; I know you're as strong as a horse, but you did look a bit pale. And the S—s, bless them, tell them I'm writing to them ... All my love, ever so much of it, to you all,

EVA

Darling children,

This is my ninth collective letter to you all. I imagine that
when it reaches you, it'll be almost the end of the year, so I'll
wish you a lot better luck for the new year than we've had in
this one! How I long for the time when we'll all be together,
and all this will be a nightmare of the past! I am quite sure
that *will* happen – that things will be cleared up and we shall
come out of this free, and laughing. For the moment, all I can
do is wait and hope. Till when? ... Anyway, meantime I'll
carry on as usual. First, Mafaldita: Thank you for those
superb pictures; I didn't think you could possibly do anything
better than the lovely one you did the day you visited me – but
now, behold these gorgeous little things! ... You have a lot of
talent. You must cultivate this particular style – it's very re-
warding – those glowing colours seem to come straight from
the warmth inside you. You know, your letters and pictures
are one of my greatest joys. And I'll tell you why. Not just for
all the love and tenderness they express, but because I can see
from the way you do them that you are *really well*. I don't
know whether I've said this before, but human manifestations
in general – the way in which one behaves and does things –
are very indicative of what is going on inside one; handwriting,
for instance, tells a great deal ... (you know there's a study
called graphology, devoted to it?) and your writing is so firm
and well-defined that it seems to me to indicate an unusual
degree of inner balance. From so much that you send me, I
can see that, even though you're going through a very hard
time, with the people you love most and have most in common

with having to be away from you, you still have great fortitude, great inner strength, a basic certainty that we all love
one another, and that nothing and no one can ever break the
solid bonds that unite us. With strength like that anyone can
face life – and you are young and have a life of great promise
ahead of you. Don't you find that exciting? Some people may
be thinking, 'Poor child, having to be without her parents ...'
and they understand so little of what is happening that they
feel quite sad when they think of you. Yet I, who love you so
much, am not sad at all : you make me feel cheerful and happy.
Because I know – I can see it from your letters – that you are
strong. Being strong doesn't mean that you aren't unhappy
at times – quite the opposite. Anyone who *feels* things – and
being able to *feel* is something very important which human
beings should be continually trying to develop in themselves,
though unfortunately the world is always trying to repress it
– has a profound response to everything that is happening, and
it makes them miserable or happy, laugh or cry, sing, or draw,
or dream ... All these things are *good*. And all this will happen
to you – and a lot more too. What is important is for you to
understand the reason for it all, and devote some time to
thinking and reflecting upon what you feel. Then you begin to
have a new kind of knowledge – the kind gained from *thinking
about what we feel*. First, one feels; then one thinks about it :
you feel unhappy for instance, so you cry. Afterwards, when
you feel better, you think about what it was that made you
unhappy, why it made you cry, etc. And you'll find you come
to understand something you didn't know before. And the
same thing applies to happy feelings, or irritations, and masses
of things that one feels and then can't see why one felt them.
In fact, something like this happened to me when I read in
your last letter, 'I've made a mess of things'. I gather you spent
the whole week in bed, with Teresita (poor dear, with a tempera-
ture and nightmares! give her my love) but that it's all over now.
You missed your exams, though you really knew the history
perfectly well – but I'm sure Josefina will make some arrangement about that. You know I've always told you that you
shouldn't worry so much about exams. They're a trial one *has*

to go through, a *necessary* stage in a process, but you must
never forget that what matters is what you know – which isn't
necessarily the same thing as 'passing' an exam. I realized, the
day you were here, that you were nervous about maths and
certain other subjects, and thought you'd do badly in them.
Darling, keep quietly on studying, and if you do badly in an
exam it doesn't matter at all. All that matters, let me say again,
is how much you know. And to *know* you've got to read a lot,
and ask questions, and find new things out, and discuss doubt-
ful points with other people. It's not easy – studying demands
a big effort. A lot of people find it too much, and give it up.
It's like gym – in the early days you get terribly stiff, but you
gradually get over that and become more flexible, faster, more
energetic, and eventually you are strong enough to do harder
and more complicated things, and you get better and better;
and that's the same as the way one grows into a real human
being. Do you think it's worth the effort? A lot of people believe that to live like human beings, to live *humanly* (i.e. thinking), is quite comfortable. But in fact it is anything but: living
like a vegetable is easy enough, but being interested in things,
and thinking about them, and acting in accordance with what
one feels and believes, calls for continual effort. But it's well
worth it, because it produces a kind of satisfaction and a
really profound happiness that's like nothing else. (Same old
lecture ... !) But aren't I right, Pablo – you, over there in
Rome? I've heard nothing of you for several days. You've
spoiled us so with your journals, and poems and reflections
that now, when we have a few days without anything, it
seems like a hundred years. I hope by now you will have got
my last two letters – one to María Luisa and the other to you.
This one may not reach you at once, because you were talking
about a bit of a holiday in the North ... In any case, I know
you'll send us some word. You asked me in one of your letters
about a good translation of *Capital*. The best in Castilian is by
Wenceslao Roces (published by the Fondo de Cultura Econó-
mica, and also in Cuba). There is, by the way, a very short book
which I've read here, and which seems to me a very good
accompaniment to it: the *Introducción a la Economía*

Marxista by Mandel (Ediciones Era, Mexico City). By the way, when you're in Rome, if you go to any of the Feltrinelli bookshops you can ask to see the publisher's wife (now his widow – he was murdered in Milan, if you remember). Feltrinelli was a great friend of ours, and we knew her too, though not so well. I think she lives in Milan, but they can give you her address and you can write to her. I think about you such a lot, and how perhaps you'd rather be with us – not because you aren't happy there, because I know the family are doing all they can for you, but simply because all that means most to you is here ... I can only tell you to wait and hope. We'll have to see how all this works out – things are still terribly confused and getting more so. We don't even know when the case against us will be ready. Yesterday the interrogator told me it would be quite soon now, but there's been a change of Prosecutor, which may delay things ... We know nothing. I feel much happier during this long waiting time knowing that you're out of the country. Do make the most of it – try and become proficient in communications studies (or whatever it's called), and above all, learn some Italian! How about your Russian? It's a pity to drop it when you were doing so well. Write to Bandrés for whatever advice you need, and also send him whatever news and press-cuttings you have. Is Pepito's office arranging all the photocopies of our letters all right? I'm afraid we've given him far too much work, but he says he's pleased to do it. Now Juan, what about you? Do you get our letters regularly? I must say, I worry a lot about that. I'm afraid of the system breaking down somewhere, and you being left outside all that's happening here. Where I am now I don't hear much news, but I know enough to realize that we're going through a tricky situation, which will have to be resolved somehow pretty soon. 'Court politics' has never been my strong point, and I really feel very much at sea as to what is going on in high places. I've always been more one of the 'common people', and I feel that more than ever now. But I somehow feel that we're not far from the dawning of a new day, when there'll be joy and sunshine, and we'll be together and free, and can all clasp hands. But till that day actually dawns, we must keep on communicating. Though your letter meant a lot to me, it seemed a bit short and hurried. I know you have an awful lot of work, and that you have to divide up what little free time you have among us all, but I would be glad if you could at least give me some details about your academic studies, and how they work in with your practical work. I'd also like to know your views about things that are happening in the world. I'd be very pleased if you could visit the Vietnamese delegates on my behalf (tell Melba), and let them know that in an obscure place in Madrid called Yeserías, there is a person who, by remembering the valour of their people, has managed to find the strength to bear all sorts of adversities quite cheerfully (it's something we've learnt from them). And I'd also be glad if you could see Beatriz, Tencha's daughter, and give her my love – we can't find out where her mother is, and I heard that she was asking after me. Tell them *all* that they're constantly in my thoughts – Cuco, Alba, Anisia, Pepe, and everyone. Whenever you talk about me or think about me, you must see me as someone who is going through one of the most intense moments of her life. Being here, I have the chance to think and reflect about my own life; about the sufferings of so many of our fellow-men existing in sub-human conditions all over this unjustly ordered world; about the best way of trying to change things; and finally about the heroic example of those peoples who are struggling with such a gigantic effort to escape from their condition of under-development. You are actually living in one such superb experiment, and that makes me very happy. But don't just *accept* things. You must remain alert – don't doze off! You must keep thinking, arguing, criticizing, and thinking all over again. It is this battle of critical thinking that we must never, ever give up. In fact it's not so much a battle as a continuing struggle, a hidden, underground war that must be waged against entropy. Entropy tends to the degradation of matter, whereas Revolution tends the opposite way, ultimately representing liberation, the overcoming of the tendency to decay. But this means a continuing tension – studying every phenomenon in depth, analysing it in detail so as to produce the synthesis that subsumes it. I really envy you being lucky enough to have this experience; I'm only sorry you can't pass it directly on to us! So, if you *can* give a few more details in your letters, it will make up to me somewhat for not seeing you for almost a year and a half. What are you like now? Have you grown any more? Are you thinner or fatter? Couldn't you send me a recent photo? There are some young girls here who long to 'see' you! But they needn't bother Diana ... Does she still figure in your love life? By the way, don't you draw any more? Do send me some of those funny little drawings you used to put in your letters (and if Pablo is still listening, the same goes for him, too). Have you still got the same flat-mates? Tell me about them – about everything – I *need to know*. Well, I'm coming to the end of the paper. And the bell is about to ring for us to be counted (the second counting of the day). Today I shall read, study for a bit, and perhaps write to Yaya. Till next week, then – the holidays will have begun by then. We'll 'meet' then, and we'll sing together. That – singing to a guitar – is a luxury we have every day. I'll be dreaming of you, all those I love in this huge family of ours – scattered yet close, steadfast and certain of victory in the end; and I'll write you another letter soon in this same tiny writing to get a lot in. As Alfonso says, our arms are long, and our hands are clasping one another's in a grip of iron, and the warmth of all our bodies becomes one. If I close my eyes, I can feel as though I'm holding you against me for a long time.

EVA

Darling children,

As I write, this Christmas Eve 1974, fate has put us all in very different (and very distant) places; I want you to know that you are more than ever close to my heart. I'll start with Eva. You have no idea of the vicissitudes I went through before getting your Saturday letter! You see, the interrogating officer came to see one of my friends, and whenever he comes he takes up a whole large room – you've been there, it's the place we had lunch – so the girl who hands out the mail from our families had to go somewhere else. Anyhow, in all the confusion, one of the envelopes you had sent got lost, and the other finally turned up in the chaplain's office. So I didn't get your lovely picture and letter till Monday morning! Can you let me know what else you sent? The horses were beautiful, and some of the others liked them so much that I made them a present of the picture to put up in their room. I hope you don't mind? It looks very nice there, and cheers them up. How do you manage to produce such pretty things? I certainly don't think you must give up art – in fact I think you should work extra hard at it. Papa tells me you sent him a very nice picture, and he is going to write a poem for you. Isn't that marvellous? Aren't we lucky to have a poet in the family, who can produce verses, and songs and ballads at the drop of a hat? Not everyone is so fortunate! And how lucky the rest of us are, in Tío Maroma's family, to have our hard-working Mafalda who gets such very high marks! Your marks really do seem to me to be excellent, especially when I think that you do so many other interesting things as well as your school work –

you read, and paint, and think ... Because I can see from your letters what a lot you think; you don't just say the first thing that comes into your head like some kids do. And it's marvellous to have been able to carry on working so well, with all the problems you've got – not being able to be with Papa and Mama, or with your brothers; you must realize that not everyone would take it with as much courage and strength of mind as you have! ... It makes me very proud of you indeed, and I want you to know that. That is the greatest joy you could possibly give us. All the things I got today have made me so happy. I see that Josefina and the teachers at the school have remembered me – and Alfonso. And I was even happier to find that they had given you so much money to buy clothes – and, by the way, what sensational trousers! Where did you buy them? And have you got your shoes yet? – Oh, by the way, speaking of presents, will you remember to bring me some red wool for Pablo S—'s cap? What about Manuela – will you be seeing her these holidays? Now, what about Pablo Sastre – what shall I say to him? The most comforting news I've had for a long time was when Uncle Pepito told me the other day that there's a postal strike in Italy. That explains why I've had no news for so long – I was getting really worried, because your last letter was dated 1 December – almost a month ago, in fact! – and only one letter from María Luisa in between, which made me even more worried. Did you go to the mountains? I feel very much at sea. I *must* know what you're doing. I read the letter Alfonso sent you – with the system you set up here we never miss a letter; it's terribly hard work, but it really functions miraculously – and he's very worried too. We really need to know more. Are you still keeping your diary? Are you studying anything new? Have you written any horror stories, any stories at all? How are you settling in? Do let us know if you have any problems or any reservations. Sometimes I'm afraid that this thing that is happening to us all has had a quite disproportionate effect on you. I don't know what to say to you. I just want you to know that I'm in good spirits; i.e. that, though fully aware of the gravity of my situation, I'm not giving way, but am waiting for things to sort themselves out, with plenty of faith in the future. You mustn't let your anxiety get you down. You must make a real effort to overcome it; it's a question of self-control and directing your energies to doing something. The problem is – what? Perhaps it would be best for you to feel you could make yourself useful by *doing something for us*. Something practical, something you could actually *feel* being useful (because in fact, whatever you do is always for our good, I know that). Might you be better off in Paris in that respect? I find Italy a bit frightening politically at this moment, with fascism just around the corner ... You'll have to think about it, Pablo darling, and decide for yourself. I sent you to Rome because I thought María Luisa's house would be so good for you; it would provide the atmosphere of love and understanding that you most needed. And Alfonso, from Carabanchel, thought exactly the same – but now, it's hard to be sure of anything ... I'll wait and do nothing till I get a letter. And Juan, what about you? I know that when our good friend arrives from Havana, quite soon now, we shall have the latest news of you. I hope you've been getting all our many letters. If so you must by now have a pretty clear picture of just what's happening to us all here. But anyhow, it has struck me that you ought to get more magazines, and I'm going to make sure that you get sent some every week. You'll see from them that there is a most impressive atmosphere of solidarity, not only internationally – which is beginning to be something quite spectacular – but even here at home. I feel very confident that things will work out; truth is bound to prevail. But I know too that I wouldn't feel such confidence if I were in isolation. Nothing makes one feel stronger than knowing one is a tiny section of a vast family all of whom love one another and are helping one another. It's like a lot of communicating vessels, passing on warmth, and love, and strength to whoever needs them. Today, disaster has overtaken me – I was quite *sure* I should wake up early this morning, and could write to you as always. But it's now almost nine-twenty, and they collect the mail at nine-thirty – and I've hardly said anything! Let me just say again to you all that

FROM A SPANISH JAIL

TODAY
Christmas Day 1974
in Yeserías
★   MADRID   ★
An old and ugly mother
is thinking, and dreaming
and LOVES you

I'll use this corner to send love to all the nieces and nephews – Aurora's and Alicia's and Anita's children, and of course, Pepe's and Pepito's. And to the grandmothers. And to all the family.

And greetings too to all our friends here, and all over the world – pass them on please (Juan and Pablo!).

The next letter I'll start in good time, I promise.

Do you remember dear old Quevedo? 'The starving people do not fear death ...' 'I cannot keep silent ...'

Juan, you *will* remember to send me a photo?

ALL MY LOVE!

My three darling children,

   As always I'm writing to you all three, but this letter will be specially for Eva; apart from anything else, because I've had no letters from Juan and Pablo lately, and without that it's very hard to have any kind of dialogue! But also because Eva has asked me a very important question. So, let's get to work on the problem, Eva darling. Suppose we make ourselves comfortable, sitting together in the sun, this bright shining winter's morning? There's a little step over here in a corner where we can sit close together, with no heavy clothes on – it doesn't do to be over-dressed when you're taking the sun! – and we can talk in peace; let's tell each other our troubles this last day of the year. You say, in one part of your letter, 'Really, it seems to me that what the family is is a kind of union for several people who love each other, and pass on their ideas and help each other. Isn't that right?' Yes it is right, in a sense; and it shows that you have thought about it – starting off from your own experience of our family. It's right, but it's not always like that. The subject is a very difficult and complicated one, and people have thought and written about it an immense amount. Over a hundred years ago, a great thinker called Frederick Engels (and you should remember his name, because not only was he a great thinker, but a great friend – which is not something that can be said of just anyone – and a friend of none other than Karl Marx – the philosopher who taught us a whole new way of understanding what happens in the world; do you remember how Pablo used to read *Capital* on Saturdays? Anyway, those two were very great friends and had a continuous correspondence and told each other all their ideas.) Anyway, Engels wrote a book called *The Origin of the Family*, and in it he explains several things ... But now I'm going to tell you what I think. First of all, it seems to me that generally speaking, though the family can be something very good, it's usually something pretty bad. If you think of most families, they're usually groups of people who don't get on well at all. I don't mean that they don't love each other, because the fact that they are made up of parents and children and brothers and sisters is enough to create strong bonds of affection; but since they don't generally understand one another very well, those feelings are blind, and they give rise to blind passions which can't develop in a really *human* way. As with so many things, the trouble goes right back to the beginning. To being free to choose your own partner: though it looks like something pretty easy it isn't, because being free is very hard work – you have to overcome a lot of obstacles to gain experience. And the more knowledge you acquire, the freer you are, but, at the same time, the more committed you are; so being free isn't easy. So then, only when you freely – in other words, knowing what you are doing and why – choose a partner, then you can begin to live together with a good chance that you'll get on well and make a success of it. That's the first step, the basic step, and in most cases it's the first trip-up. (The moment you start looking into the reasons why most people got married, for instance, you tend to find misunderstandings, superficial interests, wishful thinking ...) It seems to me necessary that there be a profound, emotional and INTELLECTUAL understanding (so that they can exchange or, as you would say, pass on their ideas). Then, after that first step, there follows, 'freely' too, the next step – setting up a family by having children. And it's vital that they have them freely too – *knowing* just what is involved, and being prepared to take on that commitment with all its consequences. When that happens, then a family starts off with firm roots and should be able to grow healthily. I don't mean there are no problems – there will be plenty, some of them enormous, but they'll be open and above board, and will in some sense point the way to their own creative solutions. When the parents themselves have become mature in this difficult job of 'understanding', they will really try to explain things to their children, listen to their questions, and learn more themselves because all this forces them to keep on thinking. In this way a group of people develops who live together and enrich one another; and this develops into a communication with the rest of the world. The solidarity of their life together is projected into the world outside, and from the world outside comes fresh experience which enriches the central group. So, the family as I see it is a kind of commune — remember, that's what Papa said — that we were a genuine commune — functioning in coordination with the outside world, and keeping a living contact with it. A group who *feel and think together*. That is the real key. And you've found that out by thinking about it ... that they love one another, and pass on their ideas to each other, and help each other. You've expressed a difficult idea very well! But alas, what happens in a lot of families is that they love each other very much, but *blindly*, and when it comes to communicating, they find they can't think together. (I'm talking about *real* thinking.) This second step is fundamental. Equally fundamental is the third step: this group or commune, called a family, must *communicate in depth with the outside world*; they must be concerned about the society around them, and understand it and interrelate with it. Of course there will still be further problems, some of them quite complicated: that society isn't always what it ought to be, and the human beings in it haven't always had the chance to develop fully so that they can think for themselves, and have the freedom that goes with understanding. Which is why we come back to what I said at first — that in most cases the family is a mess ... But the time must finally come when things are different, and more creative. Many people believe that the family can be a good or bad thing in itself. I don't. I think the family may be a good thing or a bad thing *depending on* the society it is in. And I believe that when people talk of doing away with the family, what they mean is getting rid of the kind of selfish, closed-in family that reflects a corrupt and degraded society in which people eat other people up instead of helping them. In a more just society, there would be a fairer division of labour. Men and women would have the same opportunities for work, and therefore could both look after their children. (That's extremely important, because at the moment everyone thinks it's mothers who should do that by themselves!) All the relationships would be much richer and more complex. While the parents are at work, the children would be in nurseries and schools, and then they'd all come home again – that's very important too, that continuing and frequent interchange: there's no denying the deep emotional relationship between parents and the little creature they've seen growing up day after day! Some people think children should be separated from their parents very early on, to be brought up collectively – but I don't agree. I think children's upbringing should be a combination of school life and home life. But the school must be very different from the kind we have now, and home must be a 'real family'. A Vietnamese woman once told me – it's amazing how often I find myself referring to Vietnam! – how important the family is in her country, and the tremendous role families have played in their struggle for liberation. It's easy to see why, because when a family starts thinking, as well as loving one another, the way they love one another becomes happier and more creative. As they think, they exchange ideas, and they find out the whys and wherefores of a lot of things, and gain more sense of purpose. Apparently in this friend's family, everyone was working and playing their part, and life was very satisfying. The old people looked after the children: they would tell them stories and tell them about their own lives. (Just think what a lot of things old people have to tell when they've had full lives – if no one despises them for being old, and they don't feel useless! That's another thing that must change in the new family: things must be very different for old people from the contemptuous way they're treated now. We must talk about that some day.) And as they chatted, they would also work at some of the small – but necessary – jobs around the place, so both the old and the very young could be useful. Meanwhile, the young and strong could go out and work on the tremendous tasks that had to be done. So, try and picture yourself in Vietnam – I seem to have got rather off the subject, and with all that I haven't managed to say a quarter of what I intended! It's really difficult having to get it all onto one sheet of paper! Anyway, the one thing that's clear out of all I've been saying is that what you say is *very sensible*. And I'm delighted that you see the family like that, because it shows that you're really making headway in learning about life. This conversation really needs hours and hours, because there are so many problems we've had to leave hanging – but they all revolve around the need to understand what the issues are, to disentangle them in detail, in other words, to *know* in order to be *free*. We have to come back to study the problems once we have worked hard enough to win freedom; and the more *deeply* we go into them, the *freer* we shall still become. So, step by step, we shall become freer, and understand more, and take on all the commitments of being a human being.

Eva darling, I think I'm wandering in my mind – probably from too much sun! I only wish you were here now, looking at me with your bright, eager eyes, and could ask me a definite question that would bring some sense into this conversation! It's terribly warm in the sun. Juan and Pablo aren't here, and yet they are here – how do you explain that? Now we must get up, and put on our jackets (your duffel coat!) – it's foolish to go from the sun into the shade without a coat on, remember? – Is it hot in Cuba? And in Rome? And in Carabanchel? No, I know it's cold in Carabanchel ...

Our family is really like a kind of red star: there's a single heart, and five points in different places, gazing out on infinity: a whole universe of possibilities. We certainly haven't got much in common with the traditional family, but it can't yet be said that we've become 'the new family' we hope will exist in the future. Now in 1975, we must go on talking and talking – we've still got that great luxury you spoke of at the beginning, Eva: we are united, we love one another, and we pass on our thoughts to each other. It's even better if we can say that we all together make up part of that other vast family, who think, and feel, and worry about the same things as we do. I love you so much,

EVA

Darling children,

This letter will be a bit delayed, because yesterday – the day I would normally have written – they moved me here to the hospital. Not because I'm ill, but because the General Prison Board has granted Alfonso and me the concession of seeing each other for a little while – which we've been asking for for the past month. So the reason for the delay is a joyful one! I'll be here for some little time. I have a very comfortable cell to myself – it could be a room in any modest hotel – I've got heating, hot water, and very good light for working in. I've a good solid table, and I've brought my typewriter. Indeed, as far as one can be in this situation, I'm happy; and I tell you this at once, because I know you'll be very pleased. I abandoned this letter to go to lunch, and then, after that, – I saw Papa!! Oh my darlings, I just can't put into words what that meant to me! I felt a bit shaky – I thought I might burst into tears, or feel terribly unhappy, or be absolutely shattered ... In fact, when I saw him what I did was to laugh – I felt as though I would burst with joy, and I started talking very excitedly, and it seemed as though nothing had happened at all, and everything everywhere was happy. If I had to describe it, I'd say that I got back all my pre-prison cheerfulness; and it was so marvellous that it almost *hurt* – after thinking that perhaps he would imagine I was having to make an effort not to show how sad I was! All that tremendous emotion at seeing him came out in laughing and joking. Life is full of surprises! It's made me realize how important Alfonso is in my life – how much I need him, and how, simply by being there, he gives me strength and courage. *He*, who everyone thinks of as sad and taciturn, one of life's tragedians, turns out to be the only person who can cheer me up – though I'm the official optimist of the family! It's not really so surprising. It's because he's such a wonderful, such an ideal partner, with his warmth, his goodness, his seriousness, and his profound and complex vision of life, that he gives me so much security. 'How handsome Papa is!', as my little Eva would say – with his beard, and his smile, and his grey sweater, and his lovely enormous eyes; no one could help loving him, and we've really been lucky to have been able to live with him for so long. *And* there's more to come! For I'm absolutely sure that the truth will soon become clear, and the day isn't far off when we'll all be together again in our own dear house – poor thing, all tattered and torn to shreds, but that isn't serious – what matters is us all being together, wherever we are ... Our time together seemed terribly short – but I suppose that's natural, and I'd have thought so even if it had been two hours; but I'm so happy to think there'll be more in days to come. (That's why I'm living here, so I don't have to be transported every time.) They're calling me to supper, so I'll continue later. Now, after a delicious meal of vegetables, fried eggs, potatoes, fruit and custard, I'm back, feeling very cheerful, to go on with this letter. I really don't know how to express how marvellous I feel here, by myself in this little room – which of course I immediately ornamented with my collection of all your photos and one of Eva's pictures which I brought with me. There is one corner, just above the table I'm working at, that is full of joy and light for me, with all your dear eyes like so many windows letting in hope and goodness ... Anyway, as I was saying, I'm by myself, but with such a sense of abundance inside me, and so not-alone with memories of you, and today, above all, of Papa whom I love so much. By the way, he told me a lot about a wonderful letter from Juan – which I much regret not having received – why are the copies taking so long? (That's an aside for Pepito – so that when he reads this, he'll send me one quickly! Actually, I think it's probably my move here that's to blame. You'll have to send everything here now.) Juan darling, I hope you realize how *delighted* we are to hear your news? Of course we know that it's not because you don't care that you don't write more, and I feel very proud to know that it's because you're working so hard, and preparing to be a real, full, adult human being. I rather think you'll soon be getting the journal I wrote during five days when I was in solitary confinement, and which they've now allowed me to send out. You'll see from that how strongly I feel that your lives must go on, and you must get ready for life in every sense. As soon as your letter reaches me, I'll let you have an answer – okay? As for Pablo, I hardly know *what* to say to you, darling. Not only was there the strike in Rome, which stopped any of your letters getting here, but the few that have come haven't actually got to me yet. Alfonso also told me about a card and a letter that I still haven't seen. According to him, you're very well, and everything's going swimmingly. I'm very relieved to hear it. Have you had a letter from Bandrés? Do let me know. For the present I think it's safer not to write to me directly, because I don't know how long I'll be here, so send it to Pepito. How's all the reading going? And how's your Italian?

One day we'll be able to thank them for all they're doing for you. Did you hear that Françoise has given me Freud's *Interpretation of Dreams*? It's a book I read years ago, and at first I liked it a lot. Now I've re-read it, and something of the same thing has happened to me as happened with Marx – I'm convinced that one has to go to the original, because most of the disciples either misrepresent the master, or turn him into dogma. Freud has a breadth and richness totally beyond any of the things other people have written since ... Anyhow, we must go on talking, and above all, you must go on putting your problems to me just as you always have; as you know, that forces me to think, so ultimately it's *you* who are teaching *me* things. And the same goes for the rest of you! By the way, Eva, have you received my answer to your question about the family yet? I wasn't really very pleased with it, because it's a terribly complicated subject – one sheet of paper just isn't enough; I'm sure my writing was too small, and what I said was too condensed. But it gives us something to talk about next time. Not being allowed to write more than one sheet sometimes means performing great feats of handwriting – and having a limited time has the same sort of effect. But you get used to anything : this very limitation obliges me to summarize my ideas to a certain extent, and that has its advantages, doesn't it? The great thing is to find one's way out of difficulties – not to be hamstrung by them, or let oneself be held back by possible pitfalls. There's an old Castilian saying : '*No hay mal que por bien no venga*'.[2] It's not *always* true, but there's a lot in it; at least it is saying the same thing as one modern Chinese philosopher has put very well in his thesis about contraries : everything (whether good or bad) holds within it its opposite, and that's what you have to look for. That is certainly what we must always do whenever we're going through bad times and difficulties : first, try to resolve the problem, and if that isn't in our power (though we must keep on trying!), we must see how to make the best of it. There is a great wealth of things for us to learn from all that has happened to us; furthermore we must make the best use of this time to deepen our knowledge, and understand what's really going on around us, so that one of these days, through our investigations, we'll succeed in opening new paths that will enrich human life and assist its growth. Are you listening Eva, my funny little Mafalda? I know you are. This time – unlike my usual proceeding – I've left you till the end. Your letters are lovely, and I read the last one to the girls here; they immediately thought of sending you a postcard, though in the end they didn't. But they're such nice letters that I'm going to pass them on to Alfonso for him to enjoy too, and he'll see how good your writing is, and how well you put things. Perhaps I shouldn't tell you so for fear of making you vain, but it's the truth, and as you know I don't like not telling the truth, especially to you children : you always understand everything so well that it's nice to tell you things. Your last picture was delicious. I shall put this week's one up in my new room.

---

2. There's no bad that can't turn out good.

When my letter arrives, you'll be on your way to school. Tell Josefina that I sent her a Christmas card – I don't know whether she got it – and that I'll be writing her a letter soon about you, and your schoolwork, and where you'll stay next year ... Give the Pablo S—s my love – distribute it as you think best among the grandparents, children and grand-children! – and Teresilla's family too – I hope you can some-how make them understand how dearly I love them for all they're doing for you! Oh dear, the paper's nearly used up. It's a bit late, and I'm actually writing in bed – I'll probably be asleep by the time I sign it. What are you all doing now? I wonder; I imagine you all, each with your problems – all so different, and in such different surroundings! – yet all so united in everything that really matters! ... It's wonderful to be as united as that. I keep thinking of what I was saying to you the other day, that we're like a huge heart beating in unison, shaped like a star. We're five points facing in different directions, but in the same space. We're united by the love inside the heart, and also by our goal – a wide world in which all mankind are our brothers and sisters, and we are committed to working with them and for them. Could there be more happiness than that for a family now going through such agony? I can't say any more to you tonight; I'm thinking of you and of Alfonso, and my arms are holding you close to me; I consider myself very lucky to have you all so near me, so warm, so generous, and so much loved. Good night!

EVA

My darlings,

As I sit on my bed to cover this paper with those curious squiggles we call writing, I feel as if I'd just opened a window that looks out on you all. How very odd things seem to have been recently! It seems hardly possible that we can write so much to each other and be so close, and yet have spent such a long time without so much as touching each others' finger tips! Where are you all now? What are you doing? It is five in the morning – my best time of day – and I'm sitting in bed, in a comfortable room – it could easily be in a hotel where I'm spending a few days ... I can hear the noise of the wind outside, and lorries going by, and occasionally a train in the distance ... Where am I? I told Pablo, in a note I wrote to him last week, that I sometimes feel as though we're just teasing the people who think they're holding us here: all they've really got is our skins – as for the rest of us, it's as though we all have an appointment in some far-off part of the world, and we're on our way there together, chatting and discussing our own affairs as we go ... I have strange feelings – passionate longings to see you and put my arms round you – which are transformed into images, and fantastic dreams that I have for a time, and then they go again ... But really, I'd rather have reality – it's always much better, even though it seems harder. Could anything be more of a satisfaction to parents in prison than to know that they have intelligent children going into life with their eyes open – never deceived into false reasoning or the blurring of contradictions – deeply absorbed in what's going on in the world, critical, responsible? When I don't get a letter for a while, I do get a bit worried, and start wondering whether you're all alright – and then when one finally comes, I find that each time you're better, and stronger – that you've got your feet well and truly on the ground, and that you really love life and your fellow men. So, forward march, dearly beloved comrades – the future is ours! Now, I'll turn to my darling little Mafalda – the only one of you I see every Saturday – oh, how I long for those heavenly Saturdays! – even though it's through a plastic screen ... You were a bit melancholy last time. It's the first time I've seen you depressed like that – maybe it wasn't terribly serious, but just the result of some passing upset – the prospect of a boring or not very pleasant weekend? But I'd like to talk to you about it, and there's one thing in particular I want to say very firmly. I don't want coming to see us – either Papa or me – to become a routine duty. (No, don't give me one of those looks! I know you don't feel like that about it ...) I know, and I know it because you say it again and again with such conviction in your letters, that you love us 'more than anything in the world'; and I know what it means in your life to have us so far away; there's no question about any of that. But it's perfectly human and understandable, that just as one feels more like writing one day than another (which has nothing to do with not being interested or affectionate) so there will be some Saturdays or Sundays when it's absolutely *natural* for you to have something planned; times when you might prefer to go to the mountains with your friends and enjoy yourself, go and play in the snow, for instance. You'd be a very peculiar girl if you never felt like that – what's more natural for any child than wanting to play with your friends? You must always be honest with yourself, and not do things 'out of duty', because you think you *should*; that's not the same as an obligation you *choose* to take on, i.e. after thinking the matter over, you *decide* you'll do it. Oh dear, this is getting very involved! ... All I mean to say is that if there comes a day when you don't feel like coming (and it may be a day when you love us more than ever), then don't come. Write a letter and tell me what you did, and I'll be very happy with that. Okay? We have always cherished the freedom one has if one *thinks* about things rather than doing them just out of habit, and we've tried always to *face* our problems ... That's the first thing. Now, second, and I think this is what was bothering you the other day, I think that though you feel you need most of all to come and see us, it does spoil the chance of making any other plans for the day (because your friends go off too early, etc...) and means for instance that you have to stay in Madrid. This is the point when you have to look for the silver lining in the cloud. Being bored or having fun are things that come from *inside* us, and it's the way we look at things and experience what's going on around us that makes it boring or interesting. Situations can be terribly boring for some people, whereas others pass the time quite un-boringly, just 'observing', and learning about all the things that can happen in life. When Roser and I were little, one of our favourite games was to go to a house, or on a tram, or to the beach or something, and 'observe' everything that was happening there, and then discuss it or write about it ... Sometimes, having to be with a very small cousin, or with someone older, may seem like a terrible bore – and often it is! – but try to talk and ask questions. Generally speaking, old people are alone a lot; they need conversation but there's no one to talk to, and they can easily get more and more selfish, and wrapped up in themselves and bad-tempered ... But perhaps, by talking to them, you can manage to find out the sort of things going on in their minds, and you'll learn a lot from that. *Everything* that happens around us gives us something to think about, and the subject of old age is a very important one which I hope one day we can think about together ... It would be marvellous for children if they could have a *real* relationship with old people! There are so many things they can tell us. But so many of them are embittered and irritable; they've had a life of suffering and poverty and trouble, without a great deal of meaning, and they end up with a terrible sense of emptiness: when I say poverty, I don't just mean a lack of money, but lack of ideas; I mean they've had no understanding, no real meaning to make their lives seem worthwhile. Basically, this is simply because our society is desperately de-humanized:

people are just instruments, and once they're no use for producing wealth any more, then they're shoved into a corner and forgotten. Which is why you see such an army of old people, depressed, embittered, lonely even when they're with other people, who look forward to dying almost as a liberation. It's a big problem to think about, but you can't *think* unless you have some experience to go on, until you've *felt* things for yourself. And you're at an age when you need to be *nourished* by the events of life. Just as I tell you to drink lemon juice to get your vitamins, so I also advise you to absorb everything that goes on around you. Suppose a day comes when you have to stay with Grandma? (I know it only happens very occasionally.) Well, see whether she tells you about her life, or not: observe her ... Suppose you have to spend a few hours with one of your little cousins? The same goes for that. Talk, ask questions, play with them ... You can learn a lot from children too; and if they don't say anything interesting, it's not usually their fault – it's because of the world they live in, the TV you criticize so intelligently ... Whenever you face a tiresome situation, you can always play the game of asking, 'Why don't I like it?' And you need a bit of patience, and a lot of love. If you look at people lovingly, you'll have more understanding of their problems and their mistakes, and you'll be well on the way to being able to help in some degree to improve matters. A lot of writers, like Dickens or Victor Hugo, for instance – and many, many more! – have been able to present a world of suffering and injustice because they've experienced it all themselves; and so they've made other people able to see it and think about it. In that book by Marx that we used to read on Saturdays, there are whole chapters in which the author describes the sufferings of people who found themselves having to work in the most appalling conditions; if no one had *known* about it, then a whole theory aiming at putting an end to it that has come into being since then, and as a result of what he wrote, could never have existed. See what I mean? Never shut yourself up in just one kind of world – but try to get something positive out of whatever situation you find yourself in. You'll find it makes you much happier – you'll go on being as happy as you are now, and this will just add more to it! Will you try, Eva darling? Though I really do know that it *was* just a passing cloud ... And you must realize that it didn't make me at all unhappy – I'd have been much more unhappy to think you had deceived me with a false smile ... Will you let me know how you feel about all this? Now, on to Pablo, far away in Rome – but with your heart in Madrid, wandering through the backstreets, chatting to people, with other boys and girls ... I hope you really will come soon. Meanwhile, do make the most of your time: you can study the language as a practical matter, and Roman life as something a bit deeper. What a lot you'll have to talk about when we meet again! Perhaps it'll be better if each of us writes a book, and we can hand them round – otherwise it'll be like a farmyard! I'm just finishing reading *El recurso del método* – a marvellous book by Carpentier. He's a really great novelist; they do have some magnificent writers in Latin America. If they'd let me, I'd write him a letter. Juan, I'm dying to answer a whole series of questions which I gather from Alfonso you've asked in your letter. I'm also longing to get my hands on the letter! I hope I'll be able to answer it properly next week. I must tell you that there's a woman here who has a baby boy – and he's just like you when you were born. I need hardly tell you that I give him his bottle as often as I possibly can: he gropes greedily round for the teat and gobbles the feed down like a mad thing; he flops back exhausted when it's all gone, and grunts like a little pig. By the way, I don't know whether I said this in my last letter, but the photo you sent I don't like *at all*. I think you must have been in a bad mood, and anyway, passport photos are always horrible ... Alfonso thinks the same – have you got thinner? Have you cut your hair again? On the other hand, he says your letter is splendid, and that you write marvellously and that it's a joy to see how well you seem ... Oh Juan darling! When? When? When? Yesterday I saw your father for the third time. I'm so happy that when I sit down opposite him, even with that horrible plastic between us, I don't know what to say. Usually we talk endlessly about books ... But our hearts are beating like mad, and there's a tremendous sense of excitement . . . When? When? When? Our entire life – with all its fullness and richness – is at the moment totally dominated by an enormous question mark. It's enormous, and terrifying, and it curves round us – and one doesn't know whether to see it as a scythe of ill-omen, or a huge sickle of liberation. Question after question keeps crashing up against it. But while we wait for the answer, we still continue to live. *I feel you close, I love you, I'm thinking of you.* We must all go through the world awake, and alert, and try not to miss anything that's happening there. Our song is one of profound happiness, foretelling a glorious new day when we can put our arms round each other once again!

Oh, how infinitely I love you,

EVA

Prison hospital
21 January 1975

My darlings,

What a joy it is to sit like this on my bed, with my folder on my knee, writing a letter to you! There are times when I feel as if I'm reaching out to you with long, long tentacles, and feeling you and touching you as easily as if we were sitting round together in a circle, talking over what's happened in the past few days. How are you feeling now, Eva darling? You've been worried these last few times – I can see it in your eyes, and in the way you glue yourself to the plastic screen in the visiting room, with your nose flattened against it as though you wanted to nuzzle me. (You should be careful – that plastic must be covered in germs!) I don't like seeing you like that, you know. Nor do I like you concealing your worries from me. Why don't you write longer letters? If you are worried about something, can't you sit down somewhere quietly and try to tell me about it in a letter? I hope that by the time you get this you will have received the advice I gave you earlier, and that *you are carrying it out*. Are you? You know, I had a lovely dream: Diana (the dog) was going out, with that quick, intelligent look she has, rushing through the fields after a hare. Luckily for the hare, it got away, and then you rewarded her by giving her a lump of sugar because she'd proved herself a dog of such fine feelings ... And we all – all Tío Maroma's family – went and had a good breakfast in a hut near-by, and we enjoyed ourselves tremendously ... How about that? Don't you dream these days? It's ages since you told me one of your dreams. By the way, how are those poor legs that ached so much after skating? And your cold? You must take care of yourself; for instance, be sure to drink lemon juice, it's a great protection against all sorts of infections, etc., etc. One last question I always forget to ask: Have you managed to read all Juan's letters? Have you written back? Pablo, I've just received a photocopy of a letter of yours, dated the 1st of January, just when you got back from your wonderful holiday. I was delighted to see that, despite all the problems, you are really and truly well. I'm enchanted by the healthy sense of humour you show when you describe your life, and everything you see and observe! I laughed aloud several times, it reminded me of our meals in that little restaurant in Saint Jean-de-Luz where we had such fun observing all our fellow-diners. (Remember that dear little old couple, the wife always had an artichoke? Do you suppose they still go there?) Everything you are doing seems to me to show considerable wisdom, and a lot of understanding of the world around you – which can only be a good thing ... Carry on the good work! I wish I could feel that Eva was doing as well – and I'm sure she will in the end. It would be very nice for her if you could write to her, and suggest ideas and make her laugh. She has a great sense of fun, too, but all this has happened when she's still such a *little* girl – twelve is both so much and so little – and she's so loving and sensitive! (Are you listening, Mafalda darling?) So it would be a really good thing if you could set about making her laugh – and I'm sure you will. (Pablo really is very funny, isn't he, Eva?) As for you, I honestly think you seem very well; not depressed at all as María Luisa thinks (I think it's because she cares so very much, and perhaps isn't used to her children behaving as you do, that she worries and thinks you're not settling down, etc.); you're obviously full of creative activity which, as you so rightly say, doesn't have to mean constantly coming and going and rushing around Rome. I'm so pleased. I note that you've discovered Valle Inclán – that's great! – and your opinion may be valuable to María Luisa, just as hers will be to you. To get back to *Capital* – didn't you get my letter? I told you that the best translation there is in Castilian – whoever publishes it – is the one by Wenceslao Roces. (Yes, it's the orange-coloured one.) Your father and I have now had four meetings and we both agree that it's best for you to stay where you are at present, as long as it's not too much of a nuisance to the d'A—s, bless them. You're not too far away from us, and you can also act as a bridge for Juan. Don't think this is just selfishness on our part. The point is to try, as we have always done, to deploy ourselves in the best and most efficient way. You must go on being the messenger (I call you that in my journal, which you've either got or will get soon, because I was given permission to send it by the interrogator some time ago) and draw together the threads of our world. Yes indeed, I know how fond the B—s are of us, and so many other friends, too, who keep showing their love in so many ways. It's very important for Juan to be kept up to date about everything. It's really good that you've found a way of communicating with him direct. And indeed he seems to me terrific – full of life, and good sense, and fighting spirit; some time you'll be able to live through that same experience – and he'll be able to try yours (for I think that you too are living through something great and unusual and very complex). When one is able to observe, when one wants to see and to learn, then everywhere one goes is rich in possibilities – people everywhere have plenty of problems. I wonder whether you'll be in Bologna with Magda when this letter reaches you. Though perhaps if you've begun your course at the University and you're studying at the 'Dante Alighieri' (!) you won't be able to drop it now, and will have to wait for another chance. You're certainly going to know Italy well after all that travelling! Aren't you glad you read that biography of Leonardo da Vinci? Now you can really soak up the atmosphere. You ask about Eduardo: I don't know very much – Alfonso is doing what he can to talk to him and help him, but he doesn't really seem to be making very much effort to study – even though we *all* keep urging him to. And I don't think his situation is very conducive to study, either; we'll see what happens, but he was in solitary confinement for an awfully long time. By the way, Mari Luz has been out of solitary for fifteen days now. (She was there more than 100 days – I honestly don't know how she survived.) But, let me get back to Juan, because there are a lot of things I've wanted to talk about to him that have been 'pending' for ages ... Alfonso and I laughed together when we examined that terrible photo: 'That's not my Juan at all, they've changed him for someone else.' Let's hope you can use the little camera we sent you to produce some photos that look a bit more like you; we've had such wonderful letters – I haven't yet seen the last one, but they tell me you've had very good marks, so congratulations! – that photo doesn't suggest any such thing. If that was all I had to go on I'd be very worried about you – you look desperately thin and emaciated. I'm sure that what's happening to us must have been terribly upsetting for you, especially being so far away, and getting almost no solid facts – and those you do get could be taken to mean almost anything. (Though Alfonso did try in the very short time before he was arrested to get as much news through to you as he possibly could.) But I won't believe that that photo shows you as you really are; I'm sure it was a bad camera, and it'll be different when you have another taken, with your hair less of a mess and your usual smile ... (Do you realize that in the bedroom I'm in now, I've got one of you stuck up taken when you left, and that I've got in my wallet one you sent me last spring – of you with some friends?) From our letters, and from the lawyer (Pablo will help you over that) you can find out more about our situation, and also discover how we feel about it all. In my last letter your question about anti-psychiatry was left hanging in the air rather. It's actually a very important, and very wide, subject. First, you have to ask where it started, and why. In other words, you have to understand what the role of psychiatry is in a society like ours; in ninety-nine per cent of cases, psychiatry is used to repress things. (This has been very well described in the USA and in England – and it's in England that the anti-psychiatry movement began.) It's used in business – really modern ones, of course – firms with huge numbers of workers, etc., and always for very definite and profitable purposes. There is very little that genuine psychiatry can do, because its field is becoming continually more restricted as it refuses to compromise, or ally itself with the general repression. A couple of years ago, *Les Temps Modernes*, a review edited by Sartre, published a very interesting article about this, but in fact there's an enormous amount been written about it, and if you're interested I can get some things copied for you. When one studies the problem in the light of what has been written, it becomes clear that very little of what is happening now is useful – except to show how bad it all is. Consequently, we have to start studying all the problems all over again, seeing them differently orientated, differently focused; and we must begin, needless to say, from more complex analyses of the individual and of society. (This last is *most* important.) Laing has done a lot of work on this, but really the surface has barely been scratched. It's not just a matter of examining the neuroses and seeing them in context, but the whole traditional concept of psychiatry must be brought into question, even our ideas about the psychoses. For instance, what is schizophrenia? – that illness has been described and defined by the fathers of classical psychiatry, and used to seem forever fixed – there are thousands of problems to be considered, but I think it'd be better for you to read a few books on the subject first. In so far as I am capable, I'm trying to work out my own solution. We must go on talking about it. (Oh, how I long to see you and talk, to see you all sitting round together, and talk and talk till we reach exhaustion point!) I'm delighted to see that you spend a lot of time with Pepe and Anisia. I was thinking of you all on Sunday, because I read a story of Pepe's in an anthology published by Casa de las Américas which the family brought me. And I was very touched to hear about Alba – that she gives you presents like that – my love and kisses to her children. I felt very badly about their separation, just as you do; they were such a wonderful couple, but that doesn't really mean anything – I think there are things people choose for themselves, and people's natures don't change. I remember the old man who wrote poetry with great affection, and the other friends there too – indeed I actually saw some of them not long ago : I was in the dining room, and suddenly they appeared on the TV screen, in the background – I almost wept, I was so overcome. I'm getting to the end of this letter. I want you all to know that I'm still having a wonderful time, being able to see Papa ... Here, in this hospital, there are very few people and life is very peaceful. A young girl came in yesterday, only just nineteen, a heroin addict. That's something really terrible and terrifying. I've talked to her, and she's a lovely girl, but totally shattered. Can she be saved? I very much fear not, not so much because of the length of time she's been addicted – two years – as because of the surroundings she lives in. I think we've talked about this before, haven't we? – how things like this happen, and how behind every drug-addict, alcoholic, etc., there's some major problem that has to be discovered and re- solved. (And in most cases it's little short of impossible, be- cause it's the result of a collective sickness of society.) I'd like to talk more about this, and perhaps we'll do that in the next letter. Now I must say good-bye. Eva, don't be unhappy; I've written some verses for you – they're terribly bad, but they come from the heart! – to help you follow my advice cheer- fully. Pablo, tell me something about your artistic activities (writing? painting?) and keep on as you are ... Juan, much love to Diana – if you love her and I love you, that's a good enough reason to bring her into Tío Maroma's family. When shall we have the pleasure of another letter? Much love to all our friends – that goes for everyone, wherever they are. All my love,

EVA

My darlings,

I'm really happy as I write this, and I have no complaints at all about not getting letters! On one day I got news of you all: Pablo is writing, is painting, and is happy and making the most of his time in Rome. Juan got fantastic marks, and by the time this letter gets to him he'll have finished his exams ... Eva sent me a sheet of paper with two red hearts at the top, and a long letter in beautiful handwriting and full of substance ... Alfonso is reading, making plans for things he intends to write, and hoping to be free soon ... If you add to this pile of letters my visit from Mafaldita on Sunday, and all the plans we made together, you will understand the reason why I'm feeling so happy. However, let's take things in an orderly manner, as always. Eva darling, Sunday was marvellous! When you left, and I saw you go off, in that green raincoat, with your neat little figure and your thoughtful air, I went to my room, and began thinking about all the things we've got to do together. I put up your pictures. I found the piece of paper on which you'd written 'I love you very much' (which I quickly put into my folder) and I sat down to write a letter to Papa. It is a pity you can't all read it, because in it I described what a glorious day we spent together – and your brothers would have heard about it too. But never mind, I'll say a lot of it again later on. What about you? What did you do afterwards? Did you notice when you went out that the mist had disappeared and the sun was shining so joyfully? Did you think over some of what we were saying about the house that night? Do you remember that girl who was sitting just opposite me at lunch, who was expecting a baby? Well, it was born yesterday: a lovely rosy little girl who reminds me of Pablo as a baby. What a shame you can't see her! It's a joy to watch her feeding, and my day's been spent going to look at her, and giving sage advice to the mother. (It's amazing how the situation I've been in lately has stimulated my already strong maternal instincts!) I got the thermos yesterday. I think it'll be very useful ... and I must apologize for having been such a nuisance about it, but I need hot water in the night, late – that's when I want a hot drink, and as I have to fill it in the morning (which is the time when we can heat up water) I need a good thermos, or it doesn't stay hot ... Many thanks. It was a pity you didn't try to see me, because since it was a visiting day they might perhaps have let you. I presume you saw Papa, and he will have told you about our meeting. I'm hoping to see him today, this afternoon. Pablo, I laughed over what you told me about your story, how the introduction went on for thirteen pages and you were still no nearer getting to the point ... it'll make an astonishing novel! By the way, have you read Sartre's *La Nausée*? It's a different kind of nausea from the kind you're proposing to describe, but I think they might have a certain common origin, though in your case it's not so clear. It was a book that made a great impression on me in the years after 1945, the post-war period in Europe. I think you can get hold of it quite easily, but if not I'll get someone to send it to you. That goes for Juan too: in your letter you were asking Alfonso something about that. I imagine he will by now have answered you fully and wisely, as your father always does. All I can tell you is that existentialism had a tremendous influence on us all in those years – I'm thinking in particular of a group of us who used to meet every Saturday in Gambrinus. (The Free University of Gambrinus, we used to call it, grandly.) There were Franciso Pérez Navarro, Miguel Sánchez Mazas (the brother of Ferlosio who's in Switzerland doing important work in mathematical logic), Victor Sánchez de Zavala, Luis Martín Santos (a psychiatrist and writer, who died in an accident) and a number of others. One of the key books we used to read was *Being and Time*, by Martin Heidegger; that, together with Sartre's *L'Être et le néant*, were two key philosophical works in the existential movement. An author we psychiatrists found specially interesting was Jaspers, who was part of that same movement, and contributed greatly to enriching our understanding of the problems of mental illness with his phenomenology ... All in all, it was an immensely interesting – and much needed – phase of knowledge. If any of you are interested in reading about it, I can draw up a list of good books for you. I believe – and I think I've said this in a previous letter – that one should always go to the sources, and not just read 'what someone says someone else has said'. There are two or three key books which'll give you an over-all vision of the problem. And now, from this distance, you'll have a much more critical vision than we had. With philosophy as with anything else, there are times when a thing gets taken up by everyone, and becomes fashionable. Once that stage is past, the various distortions and hypertrophies that went with it disappear, and only what is essential remains. The same thing has happened in our own time with structuralism, and various other movements. There are times when a particular way of thinking is 'in the air' – you feel it and experience it, and it is easy to get caught up in it. This makes it quite easy to understand books which are actually rather dry. Today, it takes a lot more interest and sense of vocation to read Heidegger, for instance, than it took in our day. Yet what is actually there in his work remains precisely the same – just as Kant's theory of knowledge is still the same. The only thing is that people reading it approach it with a more critical eye, and they're better informed ... Of course, if that critical eye is to be of value, it must see things in the light of real serious thought – not just fashion. And such thought progresses only by being the dialectical synthesis of the contradiction that came before; it has to grow out of a discussion in depth (for which there must be knowledge in depth) that one has with oneself – as it were. And here again we get back to the same thing: one must go to the sources. So much has been written about all these problems, but there are some – just a very few – key books, and as long as you've read them, you don't need very much more (by which I *don't* mean that all you have to do is to read!). You can learn more about Mao by reading his *Four Essays on Philosophy*, his theory of knowledge – which in all amounts to no more than twenty pages – than by reading the hundreds of books that have been written *about* him. You have to be selective, and if in doubt, *go to the sources.* (Sorry to be so tedious!) You see, Pablo, how we started by talking about your story, and we've ended up heaven knows where! Back to your letter: you also talk about what you're reading, and I see you're still excited about Valle Inclán; that's a very good thing, especially after having done such a thorough re-reading of Quevedo. I discovered Valle rather late in life, via your father who's always been a great admirer of his. Alfonso wrote some splendid articles about him (you can find some of them in early numbers of *Primer Acto*), at a time when no one knew him here (I mean his plays). I want you to know, Pablo, that up to now your letters have been getting to me pretty well. The last is dated the 9th of January, and I hope there are more to come. I'm not going to worry about you any more – in the traditional maternal way, that is – because I see that you're well, and busy, and fully involved in a really rich and creative life ... though I can well understand that people who aren't used to the bizarre way of life of Tío Maroma's family may find it alarming at times ... Carry on, though; we shall overcome! Juan, you, being involved in a more communal situation, as a medical student cum sociologist, have none of those problems ... it's obvious that your relationship with those around you will be quite different. I realize that you're left with very little time for reading, with your work and study taking up such long hours. Never mind. All this experience you're having is much more important. What I do think is valuable, when you're living through such an intense period in your life, is to try to make a short summing-up from time to time of your ideas about it; a few conclusions like that might well provide you with the basis for a book at some future date. It's an awful pity for all those day-to-day observations which could be of so much value to be lost altogether ... What about keeping some kind of weekly diary? That would be a way of saving bits and pieces of what you're experiencing. As for my life, I can tell you that things go very quietly here in the hospital. So quietly that it seems almost weird; there are very few people, and I talk to them all and know about the problems of a lot of them ... it's quite different from Yeserías. There's lots of time for things – writing, thinking, talking. Really, when I think about it, and in view of all that I see around me, I find every reason for us to go on reaffirming in our lives our conception of the world: a better, juster world, where Man can really develop in a human way ... When I listen to the sufferings, the anxieties, and the *loneliness* of the other people here – and think also of the suffering, the anxiety and all the other agonies human beings go through (of which I've seen so much, in hospitals, mental homes, tenements, etc.) I feel almost ashamed to think how well off we are, humanly speaking, in terms of personal relationships. Embarrassed for other people to find out, when I tell them, 'Well, no, my husband isn't like that ... Well, you see, my children are different ...' Embarrassed in a way, but also wonderfully content; because, in a micro-cell of society, like our family, one can see that it is possible to overthrow the established order, and that when people can develop in a favourable atmosphere of shared intellectual experience, they really do grow and progress. That's why sometimes, when people are talking about their personal or family problems, I don't say anything and I start to cry. My own fundamental problems go much further, embracing mankind in general. Our family has been for years, and still is, the practical application of a particular concept of the world: a struggle in our own, day-to-day, practice to attain greater understanding and greater respect, and to get rid of arbitrary authority and artificial rules and regulations – in other words, to humanize the family which we see to be a microcosm of the new society. And here, as I've said, the great problems, though closely connected with ours, go far beyond the frontiers of one family's life – they're the collective problems of mankind. That's why I'm so anxious now that you should all be getting a really sound preparation, a firm foundation for logical thinking. One may indeed say that all roads lead to Rome – and that dialectical thinking is a powerful weapon that can be used in every field of knowledge – from biology to astronomy. I'd like to have said more about Eva's visit on Sunday. She's filled my room with happiness – a heavenly picture of Diana the dog, coming onto the page at the far right, leaping up, with her black and brown paws in the air, and a joyful doggy smile – with a red heart like a little star on her pale brown chest. And suddenly, before she's had time to get right onto the page – her hindquarters aren't there yet – a huge butterfly has landed on her nose, and she's looking at this extraordinary, brightly-coloured creature with astonishment. There's a lovely tall flower growing up between her paws; and a brilliant yellow sun is mocking at one little pale grey cloud. What a lot of love to get onto one piece of paper! And then there's the picture of the house I'd like to have – you know, Juan, and you know too, Pablo – a house in a wood, all surrounded with bushes, in the Basque country she loves so much. I've promised her we'll have that house one day. Much love,

EVA

Prison hospital
4 February 1975

Darling children,

I'm afraid this will be the last letter I write you from the hospital, because tonight they've just informed me that I'm going to be transferred at once. I'm going back to Yeserías; it is terribly sad, because it means I shan't be seeing Alfonso, and I won't even be able to say goodbye to him – which they'd promised me I would. I saw him today, and we talked a great deal about all of you, but we were then both quite sure that we'd have another interview ... This letter I'm writing is of course to all three of you, but I'm talking specially to Pablo and Juan, because something has cropped up that concerns a friend of theirs. Do you remember I said in an earlier letter that some girls had come in here who were ill from the effects of heroin addiction? They're much better now, almost completely recovered (though I think that given the kind of surroundings they live in, it will be hard for them to go back and live without drugs), and we've talked about it all a lot. The other day, one of them was taken to see the Prosecutor, and on the way there, she met up with some friends of hers who are in prison for the same thing. And one of them, when he heard that I was here, said to her, 'I was very friendly with her sons. We went to the same school.' This boy's name was X— and all I know is that physically he's a total wreck. Who can it be? This small incident set me thinking, and I decided to write to you – not so much to give you good sound maternal advice as to try to take a close look at the whole problem, so that we all really understand it and can talk about it together like friends. If I remember rightly, Pablo once asked me some

142

questions (was it when we were talking about schizophrenia, that day in the mountains?) and I think it's a very good idea to discuss it, as we talked some years back about the question of hippies – remember, Juan? – and in fact, in a way, the two are related. (But then, what is there that isn't related to everything else?) Anyway, I'll begin with some information – it may sound a bit academic, but it's useful – about the type of drugs that are used most here, in our part of the world. There are certain plants (hashish and a number of others) used a lot by hippies, which you smoke, and whose effects – rather like getting drunk – can't be considered particularly harmful. (Tobacco and alcohol are very much more toxic and poisonous. And for that reason a lot of people think that one day they'll be legalized.) What I see as dangerous about them is that they can be a way in, for various reasons (experimenting with something different, dealers being involved with other drugs, etc.), to other, far more dangerous, drugs. However, it's very important to be clear about this, because even some doctors don't distinguish, and lump all drugs together – thus making clear their ignorance! There is another kind of drugs which are, as I see it, tremendously dangerous, and which wreak havoc on young people. These drugs don't produce any physical dependence (though, of course, like all drugs, they do produce psychological dependence). What is so dangerous about them is that they make a powerful attack on the brain. Some people who experiment once – and take only a drop – enter a kind of mad state from which they never recover, and they remain peculiar for the rest of their lives. The effects of this drug (known as 'acid') consist in certain visual and auditory hallucinations, in which reality becomes completely distorted – the general picture they present is very similar to that of the classic schizophrenias. Hence, acid and all the various mixtures containing it are known as hallucinogens. This drug is easily available, because it's so easy to disguise. Since being in here I've discovered all sorts of ways in which they serve it up. It's a liquid, and just one drop is enough for a 'trip'. (The trip is the effect, which lasts from twelve to fifteen hours, and some people never return from it. Pablo, do you remember my telling you about a German psychiatrist who was studying the effects of mescalin – another hallucinogen – and took a few drops, and how he went mad and stayed mad? During a trip you see things, sometimes horrible, scary things – and some people kill themselves – sometimes the most marvellous things, and especially things with fantastic colours in them. After the effect wears off, you feel terribly weak – often people lose a great deal of weight suddenly.) Because it's a liquid, and because so little is enough, there's a tremendous traffic in it, and it's very widespread, even among children. A few drops on a piece of paper, on a picture, in a book; a drop in a toffee, on a lump of sugar, mixed with amphetamines and made into very small pills (amphetamines are the pep-pills some students take before exams); a garment, a handkerchief that's been soaked in the stuff and allowed to dry ... any one of these things is enough, so one of the girls here told me, for 'a whole group of people to trip for months'. This terrifying stuff is very widespread among the young, because it's hardly any trouble to get: it's often actually given away the first time, so as to introduce new customers and make more money; the person selling it is often a kid trying to get the money to live and buy (and take) more of the stuff. So scruples are overcome – it seems such a small matter – and a lot of kids take it for the first time without even knowing what they're doing. Then strange things start to happen which are quite inexplicable to anyone who doesn't know what's going on ... All sorts of bizarre and delinquent behaviour, and the most alarming losses of weight, all originating from this same cause. Then there's another group of very dangerous drugs; they're much less widespread – though they're starting to be introduced – because they're hard to get and very much more expensive: these are the 'opiates' (opium, morphine, heroin). The effects of these drugs are extremely complex, and they've been described endlessly. They produce great dependency, sometimes after only the third injection you can start *needing* them *biologically*. After a couple of years, like one of the girls here, only the most thorough-going treatment can do anything (the liver is affected, there's anaemia, cachexia, etc.). Some people become complete wrecks (like this girl's boyfriend). As we all know, from films and television, they become prematurely old. When they arrived here, those girls looked like absolute vampires – incredibly thin, terrifyingly pale, their eyes prominent, their bodies like sticks. There's a kind of ritual about it all (here I find them all enormously addicted to horror literature) – it's very complex indeed, a whole world of its own. For instance, one of these girls, who used to be plump and extremely pretty, said to me: 'It was horrible then – I had great big tits – I wasn't nice and skinny like I am now,' and when I questioned her, she opened my eyes to a whole horrifying culture that's coming into being in that world. A style is being created corresponding to the characteristics I've been describing, and in that underworld, it's now *fashionable*. There's a whole underground movement – and it's good business, too – of erotic magazines and films and photographs, and special forms of prostitution, based on an army of adolescent girls, aged from thirteen (!) to twenty (after that you're too old); these kids are totally alienated, deluded to the point of even having been indoctrinated with a 'philosophy' which they expound in their own defence. (That this is a way of being liberated, of escaping the clutches of the consumer society – ironic when they've turned themselves into such pure commodities!) 'Now I weigh 45 kilos (She's over 5′6″ tall!) – if I went up to 50, I'd have big tits and I wouldn't get any work.' (She does modelling, either for fashions, or films, magazines, etc.... But always within a context calling for one particular style ...) It was all this, this complex phenomenon of drug-taking which is growing like a tumour in our society, that I wanted to find out about. On the outer fringe are people who for one or other of many possible reasons (in a sick society like ours, almost anything can be a perfectly good pretext for opting out) go to drugs as an escape – though often unconsciously, because so often the way they first begin is quite accidental: a friend gives them something, etc. – and once in that world, it's terribly difficult to get out of it. As I've said, there are different sorts of drugs (and I've left out some quite major drugs, like cocaine, and so on), and the psychology of the people who take them seems to predispose them to try things out, and experiment with different experiences so as to decide which suits that person best. Tragically, once they reach that point, they will find out that they don't want any of them, but by then they are caught up in a whole complex of interdependent relationships. These people are then addicted *by necessity*; they've become part of the network of people dealing in drugs all over the world. The need to sell means that they keep having to create new markets anywhere they can. They become small-scale dealers 'to get money, money for their own drugs and to keep themselves alive' – from those who sell five days' supply to ensure themselves two, to people who bring several kilos at a time through the customs in a suitcase. These modest dealers (to put it kindly) are the victims who swell the World Traffic, and it's they who get caught when there's a round-up. The big dealers, the ones who are really organized, who belong to the Mafia – they're never caught, and if they are, they are let out again in an hour or two after a mysterious phone call. It sounds like a thriller, but that's how it really is; and very few films have been bold enough to tackle the subject properly. In all of this – as in everything – there are the 'serfs', the people who are simply being used, the victims and the exploited; and then there are the Others: the inner ring, the kernel of the problem, and nobody ever gets to them, because they're totally identified with the politico-economic Powers that be.

.... [*sentence censored out*] ....*

This explains why, despite the 'battle' being fought, despite the many millions being spent on trying to put a stop to the drug traffic, it only goes on getting bigger all over the world. The problem of narcotics – like so many other problems – is being approached in a very deceptive way in the capitalist world: they have great campaigns on the radio, in the papers, on TV, showing what havoc they cause. They set up special narcotics squads. They organize large-scale raids ... And people are

---

* There's a film on this fascinating subject – I don't know whether you managed to see it: *Confessions of a Commissioner* it was called, or something like that; it was showing last year in Madrid.

deluded into thinking that something effective is being done to fight the whole terrible business. (A bit like the illusion foisted on the American people, when they used to show them the horrors of the Vietnam war on TV – it always seemed to be an 'Asian' matter!) What no one ever says, because it can't be said on any of the mass media, is just *where* the key to the whole thing is, the heart of the business. Lots of people are working in good faith to get rid of this evil, but the trouble is that they are only involved at an intermediate level, up to a certain limit – and if they tried to push any further than that, they'd be surprised at what they found. For the core of the problem lies in the fact that it is such good business : almost the only people who really do well out of it are the big commercial interests, and it is they who maintain the system that makes the traffic possible. (What is going on in the USA is the major example.) This being so, any attack that isn't directed at the central core is so much wasted energy – it's bound to fail. I'd like to say a lot more on the subject – I could write a long essay about it – but there's so little paper left, and all I wanted really was to let you know some of the things I've found out here. And in fact, I fear I've done it in a pretty sketchy way. There are a lot of nuances that need to be spelled out – a whole dense sociological complex calling for in-depth analysis. (But then there are so *many* things we should be analysing in depth!) All I wanted was to give you a few basic facts to go on. I must admit that it worries me to think of you all being at large in so corrupt a society that any of your boy-friends or girl-friends might – perhaps even unknowingly – provide Eva, say, with one of these things. Are you listening, Eva darling? I know you're very sensible; I could see that from the comments you made in your letter to me about the girls in your class who go to discotheques (You're right in feeling as you do, because places like that are not the sort of atmosphere in which genuine human relationships are likely to be made; people need friendship, and they aren't likely to find it there. Those are very superficial situations, and generally speaking, all anyone goes there for is to kill time), but even so, I want you to be aware of the dangers because one can't deal with a thing one knows nothing about. And let me say this to Pablo: You're seeing – and you'll see more of – an older Europe, full of history and experience, which I'm quite sure will one day give birth to something new and fine; but this period is one of crisis and disintegration, and there's a lot of confusion, and it's easy to be deluded. Try not to be; try to keep alive and alert and observe everything that goes on with a critical eye – not to reject it, but to intervene to change things, and to side with everyone who wants to see human beings fully human. For Juan, this problem takes a different form. His situation is quite different; he's lucky enough to be living in an atmosphere in which study and work are well matched, both have meaning and purpose, and provide a wealth of stimulation for a young mind. But there is still the same danger, and what is more, it's a danger you find all over the world . . . Oh dear, I see I'm coming to the end, and I realize I haven't said half the things I wanted to. This week I'll write you another letter, because on Tuesday, when this one should have gone out, they suddenly moved me to Yeserías, where I am now. I'm finishing it today, Wednesday, at five in the morning, I'll ask permission to send the Thursday letter, and we'll see if I can write again. I'll be writing to Alfonso as well – as I feared, I wasn't able to say goodbye to him. Juan, I loved your last letter – written at the end of January, I think. I'll answer it, as well as Pablo's and Eva's, in tomorrow's letter. But this time I really wanted to give you my 'sermon' on drugs. I'm sure you can read between the lines the anxiety of the everlasting tiresome mother! Oh, my darlings, I love you so much,

EVA

My darling children, My darling children, My darling children,

I'm sitting down to write to you in the early hours of this Wednesday, and I can't stop saying the words over and over again; there seem to be thousands of different ways of putting love into them! My beloved and adorable children, with whom I've gone through so much ... Let's begin with Eva. Yesterday I got your last week's journal, and discovered that there were various mishaps at Carabanchel on Sunday, so that you didn't manage to see Papa in the end. I'm so sorry, because he was looking forward to your visit so much – in fact he told me so in his letter – and I'm also sorry you had such a fright with the horses and being chased ... Well, it's one more experience in the short but adventure-packed life of twelve-year-old Mafalda! You'll have to come back on Friday (or Saturday, if he's managed to fix the visit), and try to see him every week; what with one thing and another all his visits seem to be few and far between – but don't worry, I'm sure everything can be arranged. I can't *tell* you how touched I am by your letters. There's so much love and so much feeling in them, and you express it so beautifully. And they're filled with profound reflections which make me want to take up the threads of our conversation, and really settle down to talk for hours and hours. If only you knew how exciting I find them! In the letter you sent Papa, which he read me last time I saw him, you talked about our great luck as a family. I quite agree that it is terribly lucky that the five of us have happened to coincide in this family, as you say; but what you call luck is in fact the result of the continual effort we have all made to turn Tío

149

Maroma's family into an active community cell. And it was all of you, with your questioning – serious questions, as children's questions always are – and your persistence whenever something wasn't absolutely clear, who helped us as far as possible to get rid of false notions of authority – so pervasive in bourgeois family life – and taught us a new way of living together ... It is sad that the experiment we were making so successfully has had to be cut short so abruptly by all this. But we'll carry on, and – in spite of everything – I feel just as happy as you are, because I know we really are united by something very strong that gives us the courage to go on. You must remember that you are one of the points in the star made up by all of us, with the heart beating in unison, while the arms stretch out to infinity, open and generous, and united – don't ever forget that, Eva darling, will you? Now, with a leap, I arrive in Rome, with Pablo – singular and incomprehensible Pablo to some, but not to me: I find you straightforward and perfectly clear ... What a fantastic story you've sent us! I didn't know all that language of the backstreets of Madrid – I never realized that you'd had so much experience of those places, though I did know you had a tremendous imagination. Once again, I only *wish* I could take your arm, and we could go together for a long walk in the mountains, and talk, and talk ... What a lot of things I'd like to talk about! About your story, about the problem of style, about literature in general and its relationship to life. About the book I'm trying to write, which is becoming more and more difficult because of the immense complexity of trying to present a 'moment' of reality ... Your story arrived here without any accompanying explanation – just in an envelope with '*La Vena*' written on it. I laughed to think how surprised anyone would be who read it – I'd have found it pretty surprising myself if I hadn't known something about it beforehand from your letters. I can see you're well; I know that if you can work that means you are well. What other surprises has Señor Pablo in store for us? I'll be interested to hear your views on the last letter I wrote you, all about drugs. Yours, and Juan's views too, because the moment I'd sent it off I began to feel a bit uneasy – I fear that perhaps it sounded like the alarmist cry of the old-fashioned mother appalled by the danger of drugs and painting the most lurid pictures to protect her little darlings ... It really made me laugh at myself ... I should like to have talked much more fully with you about the problem. Basically, I still think what I said was true, but I should have shown more of the lights and shades, and brought in a lot of aspects I left out. (One sheet of paper just isn't enough for that sort of synthesis!) For instance, I wouldn't for a moment want you to see it as an attack on the vast majority of people – most of them very young – who use drugs. As I said, the key to the evil lies elsewhere, and the real mechanisms are very different. The thing is that some people are taking advantage of a situation – which though more acute than usual at the moment, is by no means new – of man's more or less conscious need to reject a society he is sick of, and seek worlds in which he can be more 'himself'. Many people who take drugs have a profound nostalgia for the kind of fulfilled person they would like to be; they really *need* to awaken their blunted sensitivities and their drowsy minds; they can see the way the human race is going along the road to total atrophy. They long to be humanized – in the deepest biological sense of the word – and fortunately, a lot of the rest of us have that same longing. But we are all trying to find it by different routes – ways to change and progress – we're trying in some way to intervene to change this situation which is so horrifying. Very often people take drugs with the most high-minded intentions; their attitude is one of quite justified rejection of a society so blemished and distorted as to have only emptiness to offer; a society in which the family has become a hell of tensions, in which work (so necessary to man) is a source of alienation, and human relationships are dominated by repression and selfishness. But I'm afraid this noble intention of finding freedom through drugs remains just that – an intention: it's only an illusion of escape. For basically, and in the long run, it can only become a slavery. Certainly, at bottom, we all seek fulfilment; we all want to achieve truly human capacities to feel and think and create. And this for me is the key to the revolution – the struggle for a new order

in which things are all so regulated as to be for the greatest
benefit of mankind in general. People are not human if they
can't think and imagine, and they can't think or imagine if
there's nothing liberating about their work, and ... But I
think I really explained a lot of this in that piece I wrote about
my life on the Cuban farm, which was published by Ruedo
Ibérico, in that book on Cuba – remember? But it seems to me
that the best stimulus to resolving this immense problem is to
be found in the precise opposite (?) of drug-taking: instead of
myself individually seeking an artificial paradise, I want to
stay where I am, in the concrete reality of the world, observing
and collecting facts (information), and then on that basis *thinking*, imagining (dreaming, as Lenin said) a 'paradise' involving
difficulties and hard work, but a great deal better. 'A man is
really great when he shows what is in him,' a peasant said to
me in the Sierra Maestra. 'He's so huge that you can't see to the
bottom of him ...' And there really is no end to understanding
Man. I have faith in that creative energy of the imagination,
which can open quite unforeseen new paths. Nothing is a
greater stimulus than the continuing voyage of discovery that
thinking is. It's a stimulus far more exciting, far more thrilling
than the euphoria induced by any drug; and experimentation
leads to addiction! But, strange though it may sound, thinking
is very difficult and sometimes also very dangerous. And once
you start, there's no turning back: you're committed ... to
something passionately exciting. That's how discoveries are
made in science and in art: with imagination like a lantern
exploring the unknown throughout a long journey that you can
only set out on if you have clear knowledge to start with.
That long journey is worth far more than all the artificially
induced 'trips' in the world. I'd like to have clarified – or at
least tried to! – a lot more aspects of this problem, but here I
am getting to the end of the paper, and I've barely begun! I've
so many things waiting to be said – especially to Juan, whose
questions I haven't answered even a quarter of. On Friday, I
promise, I'll write for you, Juan; I want to talk about the
depression you sometimes feel. I don't think I told you that a
fortnight ago they came to inform me that the Carrero dossier

is now complete. So judgement could be given any day now – no one really knows anything yet ... Give my fondest love to Pepe and Anisia – I needn't even say that – they know it. I'm more touched than I can say at the way they're looking after you, Juan darling. Also my love to the S—s, to whom I haven't yet been able to write. I must stop now, because I've been down to breakfast, and now they're calling us to count us. I promise my next letter will be long. Okay, Eva? I know your dear eyes must often fill with tears. I'm going to ask very soon if they'll let me have a day with you again, you know. In March it'll be three months since your visit to Yeserías. The visit to the Hospital was a special favour from the Governor in honour of his superior ... It'll be lovely to be together again, and hold each other tight, and make plans. Doesn't that thought make you all happy? See you very soon,

EVA

My darlings,

I'm sitting down to write with a heap of your letters beside me – great long letters, *full* of love, and ideas and suggestions. I'll start with Juan, as there are some rather special things I've been wanting to say to him for several days. You say that sometimes, in the midst of all your tremendous activity, all the marvellous experiences you're having, you feel 'depressed', and a sense of needing to be with us. How could you help it? We miss you dreadfully, too, and long for the day when we can put our arms around you and hold you close again ... But somehow you've got to put up with it. You must have patience – a long and wise patience into which you condense (so to say) all your longings, and all the energy you'll need for the future when you come back to rebuild our house and we're all together again. Your job now is to study and prepare for life. The situation is as it is. And, as you yourself say, despite the pain of separation you sometimes feel, yours is a unique experience. But sometimes, sometimes you feel a bit depressed ... You wouldn't be human if you didn't. It's inevitable. One has one's understanding of the world, of one's plans, of what one is fighting for ... and one knows theoretically that it's all going forward, that history is being made, that one day men will be truly human ... But even though one knows all this, there are still times when one stops and feels depressed; and one has thousands of questions, to some of which there seems to be no answer ... (Who can resolve the problem of death? How is one to *feel* the meaning of life – however much reason can explain it in theory?) Oh, how I *wish* we could be talking about all these things like we used to. But I'm limited to the scope of a letter; all I can say is that in such moments of deep loneliness, which are very human, and are at once painful and healthy (they prove that you're still alive!) you'll have to suffer alone, because there's *no one* and *nothing* that can help you. That is the tragedy of a human life; it is so short a space within the long process of history – and that in turn is so short within the history of the universe – but the very fact of being human means that one can never stop asking questions. Try to see it in terms of what your father always says about waves and particles; there's a vast process going on of which we form a part. It's hard to think of oneself as only a tiny particle, however necessary and irreplaceable ... I understand what you're going through very well – it's precisely because you're living out so intensely this phase of your life which is so packed with experience. In fact, I can almost say I'm glad, because I'd be very worried if some superficial kind of triumphalism led you to see particular aspects of the world as some sort of paradise. The revolution is a tragedy. But in fact, it is an open tragedy with a way out, which we can move away from – whereas the other is an enclosed, squalid tragedy with no way out, in which mankind is destroying itself. What matters is to keep thinking and criticizing – and that's always hard, very hard indeed ... But it's worth it, don't you think? Of course one hopes to have company on that laborious road ... I gather you aren't with Diana any longer, and yet you still feel you need to be not alone ... I don't know what to say. You're right to reject superficial relationships. Yet deep relationships can't be made in a day – they take time, and hard work, a lot of shared experience, and difficulties overcome together ... Don't be too miserable if you don't find a girl-friend. Friendship and love aren't commodities you pick up in the shops when you want them, but valuables of a different kind which you only get in particular circumstances. (Back to *Das Kapital* ...!) Women certainly do tend to be less intellectually mature, but that's because of historical conditions, and a cultural revolution doesn't happen all at once; but when a woman does achieve awareness, then, precisely because her oppression had been the greater, she makes a far greater leap and becomes much more radicalized more quickly. Of course, for woman to become really liberated it is vital that she take her place in the highest echelons of politics (both theoretical and practical), but that's another enormous subject in itself, and we'll have to talk about it some other time. Let me answer your other question, or rather, finish off something I said in an earlier letter. As a non-philosophical book that represents existentialism, I recommend you to read Sartre's *La Nausée*. It is a first experience, at an emotional level, of a whole philosophical theory. After reading that, you'll find *L'Être et le néant* much easier to understand. But really, I think all this is part of a history that's very far removed from yours. *That*'s a history which I'm sure you'll write something about some day, because you are experiencing it (and describing it to us) with so much passion, and love and feeling. Now, for Pablo: I got your letter of the 2nd of February yesterday, and I'm afraid one letter must have got lost. The one of the 21st of December – I've not been able to check the date – is one I think I did get, but not the earlier ones. I do think the post is working better now. I laughed over the dance you went to and your description of it. 'The young have to enjoy themselves,' someone said to you – and I think I know who it was – and I understand why it made you groan. And indeed, if 'the young' were really like that, one would groan ... In fact, one's always finding that tendency to attribute everything to a particular generation: 'the old', 'the young'. People don't realize that its nothing to do with age (age does of course condition some things, but certainly not one's conception of the world); there are young people who are stupid and young people who are intelligent, young people who are fascist – that fascism you've mentioned that seems to be so active in Italy at the moment – and young people who are working and searching for a better world. And the same can be said of old people. The business of the generation-gap bedevils the whole bourgeois ideology, and a lot of people explain revolutionary thinking in terms of age-groups. Papa described a meeting he went to in Cuba when someone asked some Vietnamese people there how they dealt with the problem, the conflict between the younger and older generations – I rather think it was an English sociologist, a writer – and how the Vietnamese who replied didn't understand the point of the question at all, because it meant nothing to him. Why should there be a conflict if old and young both have the same concept of the world? . . . It's quite the reverse: just because their ages and experience are different, they can work far more effectively and in more varied ways, making the most of their different kinds of energy . . . Anyhow, Pablo, you're not old, or soured, and certainly not peculiar for having been bored (which you *never* are normally), and not having liked the 'dance' – especially that sort of a dance. (And I speak as one who adores dancing.) I don't know what to say about *La Vena*: it's a good story, much better than a lot that get published in the magazines I see here. Has Alfonso given you his opinion? He's a much better person than me to consult as to who might publish it. I'm going to read it again more carefully, and I'll talk about it again after that. I think I've already given you my first impression – in the last letter. So now you're working on *El cuchillo*. I can't wait to see it . . . I see you're working for María Luisa and going to the RAI[3] – I *am* glad. I hope to get your answer to what I said about the Easter holidays. Eva is absolutely thrilled at the idea, and everything is all right at this end. Then we'll have to consider where you should go back to – I think perhaps you should continue with María Luisa, don't you? Papa was saying that if you had nowhere, perhaps you could go to Magda's . . . There's time – though not a terrible lot – to think of something. I see you're studying and doing well with your Italian, that you're getting to know Rome, and you're reading and going to the cinema, and that you feel happy with the d'A—s . . . We're all longing for the promised photo. It will be duly put up on some blank bit of wall. Mafalda darling, you say Pablo writes to you often (see how funny she still finds you, Pablo!); let's hope you'll soon be seeing each other, and later on in the

---

3. The Italian Broadcasting Company.

summer, you'll have Juan and Alfonso and all of you together. Yesterday your letter came – it got here after the diary even though it was written before. I realize how the business of photocopying slows everything down, but it's much better to do it, because then Papa sees them too. Shall I tell you something? Last night, at about nine-thirty, I went to bed; and as it was still early, I had a stroll round our little house, hoping that you might turn up, and as I was walking through that lovely wood you painted, I saw several glow-worms, and there were frogs around the little lake croaking so loudly! But the noise quite frightened Diana, so I hurried home; and I began making some delicious soup. (I know this means nothing to Juan or Pablo, but it's a special secret between Eva and me.) Eva, I meant to say one thing: when you write, try to concentrate and have your mind fully on it. Your letters are fantastic and they make me very happy, but for that very reason I'd rather you only wrote when you really feel like it. Sometimes I've noticed you repeating yourself, as though you didn't know what to say; when that happens, I'd really rather you didn't go on. And the same thing with your visits. There are some things – things that really matter, where your feelings are involved – that should only be done when one feels one must do them. I know you love us very much, very much indeed. Even if you never wrote at all, you'd still love us. And I want – indeed I need – you to write, but only when you want to do it, and not just out of duty. Will you do it that way? Then, you'll have so much to tell us that you'll fill up the page very quickly and not even have enough room for it all, and you'll really enjoy doing it. I'm right – you'll see. And also: say things in the way you think best, write freely. By the way, that reminds me that Juan says he's doing some drawing in the art workshop, and making copies – are you really? Well, I'll say the same thing to you: freedom in art. You used to draw very well, and its important for you to study technique – it's vital to be really competent – but beware of academic rigidity. You must try to express what you feel in the form you feel it demands, and if that means looking for new forms and creating new forms, then that's what you must do. I could say the same thing to you Eva, about your drawing and painting, but you're already so completely at home there, like a fish in water ... (though it's still going to need a lot of work). One final point to you, all three: Do you know who's here with me? Rosibel, that girl from your school, the daughter of Violeta's friend R—. I think she was a year ahead of Pablo ... She's a dear, and I'm giving her a helping hand here as I'm now an habituée. She's very brave, and sends all of you lots of love. She was terribly impressed by everything Pablo did when we were arrested, and it seems that his great sense of 'responsibility' is now a by-word among all our friends. She also tells me how much Isabel D— praises and admires Eva's intelligence, and maturity and responsibility. (Don't start preening yourself now, Mafalda!) Well done! I gave her your letters to read, and she was delighted. As she's been given a fine, and her mother is very ill with cancer – she hasn't long to live – I think she'll soon be out of here. Oh dear, I've got no room left, and I still have so many things I want to say. In my next letter, on Wednesday, we'll talk again. Now, all my love to you all. (Love to Anisia and all our friends there, Juan. And to everyone in Rome too. And to the S—s as well.)

EVA

My darling children,

Yesterday I got Eva's journal, and I can see she is going
through a good period of tremendous joy and excitement: it's
full of exclamations of delight, and how good things are, and
how splendid and beautiful you all are ... Darling, it's lovely
to see you with so much life, such a passion to do things, to
excel, to *live*. Do you realize, after reading your letters (the
one you sent on Friday has also arrived) I feel as if I'd been
given some kind of pepping-up injection, and I really want to
work too! The picture of Diana is marvellous. I've put it on
the head of Reme's bed, which is opposite mine, so I can gaze
at it when I'm *in* bed. I like the way you've put her dear little
heart in red, hanging from her mouth! It's a very encouraging
sight which cheers us all up, with those loving doggy eyes ...
And then there's that other little heart in the corner, which
you say is yours ... By now you've covered this room of ours
so completely that no one would think we were in a prison.
There's colour and light everywhere, and on sunny days the
walls are so gloriously gay that I become almost too dazed
to move. But, let me say again: you must paint everything
whenever you feel like it, and without any restraint; and go
on as you are, using every medium you can think of. There's
one picture that seems to me very important: it's very
strong, and seems to show that you're entering a new phase.
I mean that landscape you brought me to the hospital – I
imagine you did it with 'crayolas' – with lions, flowers, hippo-
potamuses, pheasants, etc., all on different levels, very effective
indeed ... And the one of the horses is very good too ... I

think you should use that technique more ... But really, you must do what you want to do most, though at times it may be a good thing for you to make a bit more effort and try out something new when it strikes you, even if it does seem difficult. Are you well placed for working? Is there anything you're short of? Time? Space? I wish you'd tell me about all this in your next letter. I'm going to give you the titles of a few books with reproductions of great paintings, so you can see what they're like. One day we will visit some museums together – you'll be surprised how soon that'll be ... I see the S—s are taking you to concerts, and I'm so glad about that. No one could give you a better introduction to music than Pablo S— (junior). And you must talk to him about books too; his taste is very good, and you'll find his advice useful. You tell me that you often go to Garcés for a snack after school ... What a social butterfly you've become! What about Manuela – does she go with you? Is she still a friend you can really talk to? You must tell me about all this in your letters, because we don't really have enough time during visits. What are you reading? I'm interested in everything you're doing, and feeling, and thinking. About the Easter holidays, I'm waiting for a letter from Pablo before I can start making arrangements. In any case, you'd better get a bathing suit, I think, and an anorak or a raincoat (It can easily rain one minute, and then be sunny enough for you to swim – it's a temperate climate, but full of surprises), a good thick sweater, and a blouse or light T-shirt to go under it ... But you can sort that out for yourself. Goodness, with all these preparations I'm already seeing you enjoying yourself – let's hope it really comes off – so many plans for trips and excursions for you have ended by coming to grief! It would be wonderful – wouldn't it, Pablo? By the way, I got a letter of yours three days ago, dated end of January, in other words before the last one I got (2 February), which shows that the mail is still not too good. I see from it that X— insists on a traditional psychoanalytic interpretation – I can't understand anyone's persisting in an attitude which, if it were right (and you're not really adult enough to judge), might be damaging to you. You say you've answered her. I'm sure that in your reply you've gone more deeply into what you told her the first time; maybe in time she'll reconsider, and will benefit from what she's learnt from you – in any case this experience you've had will have been nothing but good for you, having obliged you to talk it over with someone intelligent, who interprets the facts quite differently ... When a dialogue is really carried through to its end honestly on both sides, then one's thinking progresses and things move forward. About your story, *La Vena*, I've read it again very carefully – the first time I rushed through it without paying any attention to the details. It's a very good story. What a great harangue about old age you've got at the beginning! It makes a good pretext (in the best sense) for starting off from a sensation – in this case revulsion – and going on from that to present a 'slice of life' from the back-street bars of Madrid. The prologue presents a marvellously balanced view of an experience that must at some time have made a very strong impression on you. The humour is a good healthy sign! The atmosphere is described extremely well, and the dialogue is really very good indeed. Sometimes I'm struck by the way, in your comments, you use words and even whole phrases that sound foreign to modern ears – is this the classical influence of all the Quevedo you've been reading? or Valle? or Baroja? It's just little details I sometimes found quite startling ... The ending is lovely. But do you think – this is only my idea, and you mustn't be too influenced by it! – that perhaps that kind of cursing of the old woman in the last sentence was going a bit too far? Couldn't that woman perhaps have been seen a little more sympathetically, once the strange situation of nausea was over? ... Yet, on the other hand, I suppose everyone has at some time felt in their imagination something like that wish to kill an old woman that you describe there. Anyway, as a whole I like it very much indeed, and am delighted to see that you seem to be more and more mastering the *technique* of writing. Which is *extremely* important when you're at the stage of feeling your way among various forms and styles. It's a good beginning to start from the classics (Quevedo and Cervantes – of course!)

and then break out and create new forms of your own. But you'll be finding all this out for yourself ... The only thing I can tell you is to work steadily at what you like – one can't *always* do work one likes – and not to restrict yourself, or hold back, or accept limitations ... Art – and science too, for that matter – must be free, painfully free, committedly free; the revolution has many different fronts to explore, and art is one of its most important means ... You mention the new story, which you say you'll perhaps change into a play. It sounds a fascinating subject – the achievement of awareness by a boy in such surroundings. Good luck with it, anyway! Let's hope we soon get a copy here. I want a reply – I'm sure there are several letters from you en route now – to my questions about the holidays, etc. I also want – and this is something I want to say to you all – you to put your problems to me, and then come back at me if you don't agree with what I say. Stranded in here, without any active share in much of what's going on outside, one is in danger of becoming mentally shut in, of becoming a moralist giving advice from a stand-point that is constantly more and more *petrified*! I read, I talk to the other women, I try to think and think again, but I need a sounding-board – *you*, the sounding-board I'm used to (which we were all used to) as a point of reference, a guide to steer my course by. I sometimes feel furious with myself because I can *see* myself being pompous, posing as an expert, holding forth to you about this and that, and what is good (when it isn't), and what is better here than there ... I'm afraid, like Pablo's poor old woman, you'll be saying, 'Get out'. You must never feel you've got to accept anything I tell you; all I want is for us to exchange ideas, for me to learn things with you, and give you something too – if I've got anything to give. As you know, I always start from the fact that all of us have a lot to learn, and also something to teach as well ... Juan, do you remember that lecture on all we had learnt from the peasants on the farm? I've been re-experiencing that kind of atmosphere a lot lately. You know I now share a bedroom with Marí-Luz and her mother and Reme. Encarna is a very intelligent woman. Her insight is amazing – the way she sizes people up, and situations, and she does it all so quickly too. And it's amazing how well she expresses herself, how marvellously she describes life in her village, and recounts things that happened, and interprets it all. We're continuing to read *Capital*, and she sits there, but, 'Don't pay any attention to me,' she says, 'because I don't understand anything like that. I'll just listen.' Yet in fact, she brings a whole new dimension to it. She keeps interrupting to ask questions, or to add some telling experience which brings the struggle of the workers' movement right into our own day; and she finds the book so moving – something I was missing in *Capital* this time! Do you remember how some parts of it moved us so when we read it for the first time? That sense of oppression, the outrages, the exploitation of human beings who sell their work and suffer so – so marvellously described in some chapters that we read it almost with tears in our eyes ... And how one moves on from that (necessary) emotion to understanding the reason for it all, and the importance of making a really profound study of it so as to be equipped with really solid, scientific and irrefutable arguments to support the weighty reasons that impel us to fight for a better world in which people can really be human. Now, once again, with Encarna's contribution – 'I don't know anything, I can only say what I've been through myself ... It seems to me that he knows what he's talking about' – we've got rid of a lot of the mystification and the taboos, and the problems and obstacles so many people attach to the interpretation of this book (which obviously contains all sorts of possibilities for development, and can't be entirely taken in in one reading. *And* pitfalls). What are you reading at the moment, Juan? It's a rather funny question, because 'the moment' develops into two or three months waiting for the answer – and that's only if everything goes smoothly. I hardly know what else to ask you! They told me the other day that there'll be a bit of delay in getting your letters from now on, but I'm resigned to that, because I know they'll all arrive in a bunch. I imagine the same thing happens to you? Oh, non-communication, within non-communication, within non-communication! Can there actually be such a thing as real human intercourse? You talk of the Atlantic as a barrier ... For me Yeserías is a kind of island lost in a boundless sea – even though from inside here, at this moment, I can hear the throbbing of the city: factory sirens, cars' hooters (there are traffic jams regularly about 200 yards from here), a mixture of human noises, and the trains from Atocha ... So near and yet so far! There's a bird (I don't know whether it's little or big, crazy or just very young) which sits above our window every morning, at about seven-thirty, just as it's getting light, and makes a hell of a racket. It *must* be mad to settle in this yard where there aren't any trees, between the brick wall of the building and the cement paving; it wakes us all up – only some sort of monster could be acclimatized to the pollution surounding us (though some see it as a hymn to the advent of spring – it all depends on your state of mind, and how life is going!) It makes me terribly aware of the confined state we're in as we talk ... It's very hard to enrich a monologue! Let's hope we'll soon be able to talk together, somewhere in the world. We've got so much to say to one another, my darlings! I love you so much, so very much,

EVA

My darling children,

I'll start this letter with the news I was told a few hours ago by the lawyer – that the Prosecutor who was in charge of the indictment for the death of Carrero has withdrawn, and asked that it be handed over to the Military Court. This isn't at all good, I fear, because the Military Court is always much tougher, and one has less means of organizing one's defence. But to tell you the truth, though its going to make a considerable difference to me, I wasn't really surprised. I already knew that was what the interrogator wanted, and by now it really seems quite natural. For five months there's been a fresh problem every day (an interrogation, a confrontation, a transfer, some book attacking us); whenever there seemed such a *mass* of complications that one had reached the end of one's tether, something new would happen – proving that human beings have quite unsuspected reserves, and that in spite of it all one manages to carry on and even keep reasonably cheerful ... (What amazing things human beings are!) Alas, I fear that I'm going to be right back where I was the very first day – not knowing whether it's beginning all over again, whether they'll have a whole lot more lengthy interrogations on such absurd subjects as 'just who is *behind* the family of Tío Maroma', or 'why we call Eva "Eva-berri" ',[4] whether the inquiries will be rapid and judgement given soon, or whether it'll drag on indefinitely ...

---

4. 'Eva-berri' and 'Eva-zarra' (see p. 171) are nicknames for the two Evas, meaning New Eva and Old Eva. '*Berri*' and '*zarra*' are Basque endings meaning new and old. [Ed.]

Questions and more questions that I ask myself during this endless waiting – I have to develop some sort of armour-plating if I'm to keep on thinking and working. I'm working on the same thing, from all sorts of different angles: the very complicated novel I told you about, for which I'm incessantly making notes, and trying to set in order some of the things that worry me about my own life, and so on. I'm beginning to be obsessed by one thing: time – how can I make more time? During the day it's very hard to structure one's time. This being a transit prison, there are always women coming and going, and news to hear, and jobs to do, and problems to discuss, and a hundred and one excuses for not being able to concentrate. So I work early in the morning – sometimes I get up at three, sometimes four, sometimes a bit later ... That's when I'm happiest, when I can think about a few of my problems, and write to all of you (as I'm doing at this moment!) ... But it's not long enough. I keep feeling that a lot of the wealth of experience going on here is eluding me, and will be lost forever. And it bothers me, because I should like to 'bear witness' to all that we're going through at present – it's such an extraordinary, *bewildering* situation – but one can't just leave it at *that*: it really needs to be understood in depth. It's an experience from which there's a lot to be learnt in general, and it'll help us in the future because it may well happen again – though it's not exactly an everyday occurrence ... I've thought about starting a diary, and I'll do that, but I'm afraid it's rather late now, because there's all that's gone before. What a lot has happened in that five months! When I try to remember it all, and put it into some kind of shape, I can't – I simply haven't got the means of expressing it. Every time I start, what I write seems totally inadequate; I wrote somewhere once that reality *can't* be captured in all its richness – if something of it comes through it's sheer coincidence. But never before have I felt so forcefully my *inability* to express something and my *need* to do so. How, for instance, does one convey the full complexity of the grotesque, the tragic, the macabre, the ridiculous, the sublime, the crazy all coming together in one 'moment of time'? The kind of shock when two completely different worlds meet in the same situation, and strike such sparks that things that are hidden in ordinary everyday life are suddenly illuminated? It's this problem that Alfonso was presenting in his 'multi-level tragedy'. I keep seeing possible new forms of expression, and exploring and experimenting, but I don't seem to get very far. So I continue to make endless notes, wherever I am – I'm determined to succeed in the end. More than ever I'm faced with the problem of finding the *appropriate* form, the form *demanded* by the thing I'm trying to express. When you read this, though, don't think I'm trying to escape from reality and take refuge in literature; on the contrary, I'm trying to open my eyes and really absorb what I'm experiencing. And, as I was saying a while ago to Alfonso, it's not ideas I'm short of, or a sense of wonder in observing it all – it's that I simply haven't got the vitality to capture all these events in a book. *How* I'd like to be able to discuss with Pablo the whole problem of how to express things – now that he's so involved with exploring new forms in his stories. Another piece of news the lawyer also gave me was about the disgraceful book that's come out which talks about what happened in the Puerta del Sol. It's written by a police journalist – (she admits it herself in the prologue) and is based on the horrific reports published in the press at the time – in other words, solely on police accounts. It's absolutely libellous, and some people are going to sue the author, but I don't myself think it's worth the trouble. I know the enemy too well, and nothing that comes from them can affect me any more – as I've told you often, I'm prepared for anything, absolutely anything, from that quarter. In fact the woman who's written the book works for *El Caso*, and one way and another they can really get in among the people and create 'public opinion' ... What is so maddening is that we are helpless to defend ourselves, being shut up in here. I know that ordinary people see much more than they're often given credit for; they aren't so easily deceived, and they still have a critical sense, and can use it at times like this. But all the same the printed word does carry great weight – something that is there in black and white for all to read gradually sinks in. It's five months now since they began this savage campaign against us, and though we're waiting for the trial, when it'll all be cleared up, that isn't enough. Who's going to unsay all the attacks, all the calumny and abuse that's so monstrously come pouring out from all the mass media? This isn't just a bourgeois wail over my loss of respectability, either! What I can't bear is the collective deception; I grieve for my people, the ones who so avidly read the scandalous weeklies, the daily papers, or sensational books like this. *I've* got no platform to defend myself from – there's no way I can ward off this abuse, or contradict it. I feel it's very important to say this to you, because both Juan and Pablo are abroad, and you may not understand what the atmosphere is like here, especially you, Juan, because it's so very different where you are. (Mafalda is of course just beginning to enter this terribly complicated world) ... I want you to know that this is something I've been terribly worried about ever since I was first arrested – the whole business of information being distorted and public opinion misled. As you know, it's a subject I've been obsessed with all my life; to me information – using the word in its fullest and deepest sense – is a foundation stone of human development, something absolutely indispensable to the development of intelligence. Without correct information, one's thinking is based on premises that can only lead it into blind alleys ... One can only make progress if one has true facts to deal with which enable one to make proper scientific analyses. (Do you remember what I said to you when I was talking about imagination? Or was it to your father? I can't remember.) ... Hence my insistence, my obsession, over the problem of information ... Hence too the anger that takes possession of me, here, locked up as I am, with no possibility of defending myself at present except being as patient as possible and keeping my self-control: waiting and hoping for better times, and for some wind of freedom to sweep into this stifling airlessness. You can see why it sometimes makes my head ache, can't you? I could just not have written to you today, but that would have meant keeping one whole area of my prison life hidden from you – those grey, lethargic, angry moods that sometimes last a whole day, the sort of day when you wish you hadn't ever got up in the first place ... But you must know everything that happens to me, just as I want to know all about you ... At nine this morning I got a telegram from Bandrés – telling me that he's put in an appeal against this change of jurisdiction. It's cheered me up a bit. He's a man who gets things done; he's very efficient and really knows his job, which gives me considerable confidence; and he is a marvellous, warm human being too. I still think I'm a lucky woman, even in this – for the moment – adverse situation: I've got great friends, a good lawyer, fantastic children, and a husband I love. As Alfonso says in that marvellous sonnet: 'It's we who are free and they who are the prisoners ...' All we need is just a little while to be together and hold each other close, and then we'll go our separate ways freely, won't we? I've been writing this letter in spurts. It's now five a.m. on the 22nd of February. I'll be seeing Eva in a few hours. What sort of picture will she bring me? We spend the whole week here looking forward to that present! We consider possible places to put it up on the wall, but we can't actually choose one until we see what it is like – like everything else, this has to be decided on the spot. We'll talk a bit through those plastic panels with all the little holes, we'll watch each other's every gesture, and then it'll be over till next Saturday. But soon, in March, we'll be able to be together again – how I'm longing to put my arms round you, darling! Pablo, have you finished your next story yet – the one you told us about? I still haven't had any answer about the Easter holidays. I presume it's all right with you, and at this end Eva is getting very excited. I can't understand why the letters are taking so long! It's over a month since I wrote about this ... I'm expecting to hear any moment. I know that letter of mine will get to Juan, but God knows when ... Or perhaps it won't? Our traveller-friend might come any day now; I'm making up a bundle of letters, and they'll get to you in five days ... Do you realize that that great packet of letters I was keeping so carefully was confiscated by the Military Authorities? They were the letters you wrote to us in '73 and '74, and they've been subjected to the most minute investigation! It seems that the 'family of Tío Maroma' is supposed to be some kind of collective code-name concealing every kind of danger – as is my being called 'Eva-zarra'. And they also seem to be bothered about our Algerian friend (the one we call Moro); in fact I'm afraid they've even been to see him at his medical practice in Algiers. The whole thing is turning into something quite unbelievable. I feel as though I'd become a character in someone's paranoid delusions – caught up in some crazy mechanism that might end up *any-where*. They've even reached the point of saying that I have hypnotic powers, and that when necessary I can exercise influence on people miles away ... Did you realize that? However, as I said at the beginning, I've developed my own armour-plating, and I intend, *not* to run away – let me make that clear – but to use literary investigation as a means of getting deeper into certain areas of this reality I find so compelling. And then you hear nonsensical things, like when they said I carried poison with me in the car (Do you remember, Eva, when we were painting that skull on the brandy bottle, and wrote 'Poison' on it, to stop people drinking it?) and they even appear in the papers, it astounds me. I smile sadly inside myself, and keep on saying over and over that this is a time for hope, for standing firm, for patience, and, as I've said before, better times will come. Of course they will! Oh my darlings, how happy we shall be then. I love you, I love you,

EVA

very important letter

Yeserías
23 February 1975

Darling children,

I dreamed last night that we were all together in a shady pine wood, gathering mushrooms. Then, we went back to Miraflores in the old Fiat. We were all *so* happy. Not a very mysterious dream! We are all longing to be together again some day – but what is a bit odd is that I still feel so very fond of that dear little car, so useful to us for so many years. I've spent all this morning thinking about it. Do you remember it? Nice and yellow, with its black hood and its little round behind, and its wheels turning slightly inwards as though it was waiting, a bit shyly and a bit suspiciously, but still always on the alert . . . always ready to sound its horn and set off – anywhere, any time . . . And what a life it had, that fast little car! Think of all the journeys we made together, all squeezed in among our rucksacks and bundles; that car fitted us like an old shoe . . . If I shut my eyes I can go back to that trip through the mountains, exploring the sources of streams from little local roads – how many children were there? Six, I think . . . six, and myself as chauffeur . . . And those winding passes in Teruel – and how even today there are echoes of the war in Teruel – and the Pyrenees, from the Mediterranean to the Atlantic, and Galicia, and Asturias; that marvellous mining valley – do you remember it, Juan? – and all the other villages of our incredible peninsula, and the people, and the long conversations we had in the inns in Las Hurdes; then Portugal, and a bit of Andalucía and then Catalonia. We took it all over Europe . . . We really have covered a lot of the map together. And how we laughed! At least that's what stands out most in my mind everywhere.

Indeed it was a valiant little car with a long life story; an adventurous, quick, imaginative, daring little car! Remember how it held the road in the snow, and didn't skid, even without chains? It had over two hundred thousand kilometres on the clock – several times round the world! and never had a bad moment; it never had indigestion, never left us sitting by the road, never even had a flat tyre at an awkward moment – and always so cheerful, with its little yellow eyes and its indicators at the ready, and so contented and obliging. If ever it were to open its bonnet and tell all it knows ...! But we needn't worry – it's discreet and it loves us. Some people used to call it Lenin, in recognition of how hard it worked; and we loved it so dearly (do you remember, we felt like offering it lumps of sugar to show our gratitude?) that we used to think it deserved a loftier fate, and that its abilities as a revolutionary car qualified it for great undertakings. I think it was Juan who thought we should give it to the Vietnamese – I'm sure it would have acquitted itself as well as any bicycle in the jungle – and we certainly could have paid it no greater homage than that. But, alas it has met with a very different end. We'd lost track of it during those last months – God knows what it was doing! – and just the other day the Comandante informed me very seriously that it was in his keeping, well guarded; they'd picked it up in some street or other ... So it too has suffered from the ill wind that's blown us all over. Poor thing, I can just see it crouching there, imprisoned against its will in some military car park or garage, all surrounded by great luxurious official limousines, so tiny, so rickety-looking (though of course its engine is terrific) and *so* old ... It is without any doubt a very fine car, everything a car should be, without a drop of vulgar oil in its veins. And I can't believe that so full and useful a life can really end in such obscurity. I'm sure that under all its rage and frustration, it's working out how to escape from the fix it's in. I have very loving thoughts about it, and I'm sure that one day we shall get it back and cheer it up, and ask its forgiveness. Don't you think so? In the distance I can hear the concert they're broadcasting on TV – it's interrupted my daydream, but what a vivid one it was! ... All our

travels suddenly came back to me in a great wave – the whole
of that past period ... Eva darling, I've re-read your letter, the
one you talked about yesterday in the visiting room; you said,
'You won't like it, I'll write you another ...' – but I liked it so
much! What did you think was wrong with it? Was it the
amount of time you spent praising the delights of the mountains and skiing? I enjoyed that very much, because I went in
among the pine trees with you, and I sped behind you down
the *pistes*, and I found it very tiring trudging back up the slope
again for the next downward run! *Of course* I understand how
you adore it! And I can see, though you are too tactful to say
so, how very much you want some boots. Well, you must buy
yourself some. You aren't one of those girls who take things up
enthusiastically and then drop them. You must get the boots
you like most, bearing in mind that they should be good and
strong ... But you know that already. You'd better try to get
them big enough to do for next year too. Okay? Today dawned
bright and sunny, and I imagine you'll have gone up to
Navacerrada. What a lovely time you'll have there. I love the
enthusiastic way you describe everything you see, and all the
things that happen to you; and that was a lovely dream you
had, when we were all waiting for you at the bottom of the
piste. As you must know, dreams express our wishes – and I
often dream of you, too, with a happy ending. A happy ending I'm *sure* will come, so you mustn't worry. Meanwhile, you
must watch and observe everything that goes on around you,
seeing, feeling, dreaming, and go on putting it all down in your
diary and in your pictures. (That holiday landscape of people
skiing that you sent me a couple of months ago that I have
above my bed is such a joy!) And in fact, you'll find that expressing yourself like that helps you to compensate for the bad
things in life (the friendship you long for and can't seem to
find, the difficulties you come up against in your relationships
with some people, all the minor problems which are a normal
part of life but which sometimes assume gigantic proportions).
I notice you're still thinking about the dear little house we
want – we must see what Pablo has to say when you get together and you tell him all our plans ... It's lovely to think up

plans, but it's best to base them on possibilities! ... then they aren't just an escape and a way out, but a help in actually making things become what we hope they'll be ... Pablo is the supreme dreamer, and he'll explain what I mean much better than I can – and he'll explain it in that humorous way of his that you like so much. I think I'm looking forward to your meeting even more than you are – but you and I will see each other several times between now and then. And – oh joy! – we're going to see each other properly, in here; Reme and I have now been given permission for our daughters to come. I'll ask for the 8th of March, if that's all right with you and you haven't got any other plan that day – it'll leave you with Sunday free to go to the mountains. I've decided that it's better for you not to have lunch here, but to come at one, after lunch, and stay till six. That way we shan't waste time laying tables, etc., and we can spend the whole time on our own, talking and strolling round. Is that okay with you? The mere thought of it makes me want to leap and dance ... Now I'll leave that, and go on to Pablo – though this is for everyone, too. I've just finished reading a very interesting history of surrealism, a book by Breton. I don't know if I've spoken about that in a previous letter – but I don't think so. I enjoyed it a lot. I knew a bit about surrealism, especially in relation to painting, because when I was very young my father used to talk about the movement very enthusiastically: I have vague memories of hearing him giving impassioned accounts and explanations to Yaya about the possibilities it opened up ... And I knew something of the literary experiments, automatic writing, etc.; but I knew nothing at all about the position the movement *as such* had taken in relation to historical events, and to the revolution. It is extraordinary to see how on every occasion they aligned themselves with the revolution, and how they were persecuted and excluded by the Parties because they were so suspicious of anything experimental. Once again – it's the same old problem – the key, burning problem of the Revolution: the 'culture-gap' between the revolution which presupposes a change in methods of production, and the bourgeois ideology of most of the revolutionaries. Just one of the many tragedies that arise within the revolutionary movement, which, because it is so young, hasn't yet created its own ideology. That's why it's so important to think *in* one's situation, to re-state the problems continually, to be always on the lookout, prepared to look squarely at anything that isn't clear, to break boldly out of the conventional frameworks again and again, and not be afraid to explore new paths, to use one's imagination, to experiment ... It's tragic, horrifyingly and agonizingly tragic, how many opportunities are being lost. Revolution means a setting free of energies in every field, a rich creativity; it doesn't allow of *any* form of repression. Boundless liberation, which becomes a liberating 'synthesis' in its turn: 'Something you can't see to the bottom of, because thinking leads to more thinking, and there's no saying how far it'll go ...' as that Cuban peasant said to me – do you remember? – Can there be any dream more glorious than imagining what human beings will be like when they begin to fulfil themselves at a truly human level? It's terribly important to be aware of the immense wealth that is within every human being, and what a creative force that represents if it can be set free. It's hard enough to seize power, but that's a mere bagatelle compared with the gigantic effort needed to come to grips with the Revolution afterwards, in all its aspects, in all its complexity. And what makes it hardest of all is that we are all soaked up to the neck in outworn, inadequate ideology ... – that's a major point we all too easily forget! – that turns into our own 'enemy within'; to begin with we're stuck with the same vocabulary, in which it's very hard for us to make words *mean* anything, and which we've somehow got to clean up. That's why I always insist that the best way for us – in so far as we can – to combat evil (*there*'s a meaningless word for you!) is to recognize it, to get right inside it scientifically and analyse it ... There's good reason for urging people to read *Capital* thoroughly (a basic text, exciting not only for what it explains in so many words, but also for all it suggests beyond that). It really is *the* argument, the solid foundation on which all that one has so often felt is built up into something clearly understood. You feel yourself treading on firm ground, on the right road, in a position from which you can be completely open-minded and unafraid; you feel an unlimited confidence in man, in *Humanity* struggling to realize their full grandeur. So never be afraid to delve deep, to find out things you weren't expecting, to give free rein to your imagination. It's not easy to be human, but it's well worth the effort; and the difficulties come from the adventure itself, and adventurous is what you have to be to try. You can't do it without experimentation, careful calculation, hesitations and mistakes. And always, there must be freedom – in art, in science, in everything. The criterion for designating something as being valid for mankind in general will be whether or not it contributes to the enrichment of human progress. Oh dear, the bell is going for us to be counted – they've got to prove that we're all here and no one has escaped – I'll have to run along, but really I'm still with you : in a sense, I *have* escaped ... We had lunch, and then quite a long siesta time, and I wasn't able to get back to this letter, so it's taking me all day. I intended to say something about surrealism for Pablo, and in the end I've gone from one thing to another; but this is a subject that interests him very much, and Juan too – it's a great subject for discussion in view of the fevered activity you young people have been indulging in in this new society you are making such efforts to create! Will you write something on these lines to me? By the way, Juan, there's a book I'd like you to get – I don't remember whether you managed to read it in Madrid when Papa was translating it. Peter Weiss's *Hölderlin*. I mention it to you because it seems to me a most impressive book, and one we must talk about at length one of these days; but during these five months, I have thought back to it and been deeply moved, moved to tears; I especially remember certain scenes – when Hölderlin is presented by the professor of psychiatry to his students, for instance, or when a group of young people recite his poems actually under his tower and make them mean the opposite of what he meant by them. It says a lot about powerlessness, and indeed about a great many things. Do reply soon, because if you haven't got it we'll send you a copy. Pablo *has* read it, I know, I remember him doing so. Mafalda darling, when you sometimes come to something you don't completely understand in my letters, don't worry. Ask us and we'll explain, or at least get used to the idea that there are a lot more things you'll be finding out about one day, and that'll go on being true all your life! My love to everyone – Anisia, Pepe, Cuco, Alba ... In Rome to all the d'A—s, and especially to that wonderful mother who has adopted Pablo ... Also to the S—s. Much, much love. I'm finishing this off on the morning of the 24th; there's really nothing to add. It's a grey day and very cold, really wintry, mountain weather – you know how the Castilian plateau feels like Mongolia! ... I think you were lucky with the weather yesterday, Eva – it was so sunny, you must have had good skiing. You'll tell me all about it in your journal which I'll hope to get on Wednesday ...   Much love,

EVA

My darling children,

I'll start with my little Mafalde – the journal that came yesterday did a very poor job of hiding how terribly unhappy you feel. Let's see that poor little face, and your eyes, and your sad expression! 'I'm managing badly with all my problems,' you say, and on each day this wretched feeling you can't shake off shows itself in some form or other ... Oh how I wish I knew how to help! But there's very little I can say; my advice wouldn't be much use to you, because depression like that depends on so many things – it's so unaccountable ... And there's nothing I can do about the major problem that's causing it all. But I do assure you that things *will* clear up, Papa will soon be out – that isn't a lie, I never lie to you, and he will be out soon – and I'll get out too, though it may not be 'for a while', as you say so sadly. Not for a while? Why is it so long? With a case like ours you never know when it'll end ... It's always full of surprises, and we may well be set free just when we least expect. There's no reason why we shouldn't be. Now let's see your face again – cheer up, my darling. I've re-read – for the seventh or eighth time now – the journal you wrote during that rather wretched week, and how I wish – how *desperately* I wish! – I could run and hug you and assure you that it'll pass, that these are bad moments, but nothing more: they're *moments*, and other, better moments will come, you'll see ... A bad mark in maths? That doesn't matter, it doesn't matter *at all*. On the other hand, you went to a concert, and music can be a wonderful help ... And you went skiing, and you've been reading ... but, but, but ... Do you understand – unhappiness is like a black cloud passing over your spirits: things are just the same as they always were, but one is so cast into shadow that they look quite different. Don't be too miserable – there are some good things even about depression. Sometimes it helps you to see better, to see deeper; it can be like a kind of dark well out of which you can draw up strength and energy to carry on; you'll see how soon the sun shines again. Poor Juana! I can quite understand how you hate it when they all laugh at her; you were worried about that last year, and even earlier ... But that's how it is; she's very different from everyone else because she has a lot of personality, because she's out of the ordinary – despite her age, she's not just a typical 'old lady'. She's interested in everything, and she's got more curiosity about life than a great many young people; she's independent and she's free. All this appears eccentric in a world where everyone acts out of habit. Don't mind if people laugh at her; in spite of that she's a happy person, and out of the usual run of mediocrity. 'What can I do?' you ask. Well, the fact that you see what is happening is quite a lot, to start with. One day teachers like her will no longer be the exception – think of that! One day, as children grow up they won't lose their childhood simplicity, their avid enquiring gaze; today everything around serves to corrupt all that. You're better placed than many to find the answer: it's certainly important for us to talk about it, but I know no more than you do; like you, I wonder, 'What can I do?' At least there are two of us asking the question, and there must surely be a lot more people. So you see, you're not alone! There are so many things one wants to know, and often there seems to be no answer. But don't worry, there's nothing wrong with that, in fact it's the opposite: it shows how alive your mind is. Let's see that sad face now! Don't be so worried. *I'm quite sure you aren't just doing things out of duty* – when it comes to matters of feeling and love it simply isn't possible – so forgive me if I say yet again that you must always feel absolutely free when you show those feelings. I was forgetting one very important thing I've been meaning for some days to say to you: it's about words. There are some words you use, and though *I* know perfectly well what you mean by them, they are a bit unusual. Very strange things happen with words. Because they're there, and we only have to take hold of them in order to express ourselves, it ends up in each person taking them, and using them to suit their own needs. Consequently, what with being bandied about from one person to another, words gradually change their meaning, and the time comes when they become a kind of Pandora's box. When they can be used to say so many things, they can hold so many different meanings, that they aren't much use when we really want to say something clearly. We have to dust them off, take off their wrappings or their disguises, and then we can really handle them properly; otherwise they turn on us, and deceive us, making us say one thing when we thought we were saying another. When I see you, I'll explain this to you better, but I just wanted to mention it now for fear of forgetting it. And we must talk about the way some words have become a bit of a joke precisely because they are used to express meaningless things (honour, duty, betrayal, etc. . . .) or which only mean something if you look at what's behind them. 'I'd feel I'd let you down, if I didn't write to you,' you say . . . It's this that I want us to get to the bottom of when you come . . . By the way, you know I've now got permission for that? I think I told you in my last letter. We'll have a good laugh; and we'll really *do over* some of those pompous-sounding words that seem to be saying so much and are actually saying nothing! It's quite a subject – the use of words. Don't you agree, Pablo? Yesterday I again read your letter of the 9th of February. I see that Bologna is settled. So you'll meet Eva there (nothing is fixed yet, but I'll let you know when it is), and after that what you'll do is still in the air. What do you think? I think it might be best for you to stay in Rome, perhaps in a *pensione*, and continue with your Italian etc., and finish the year's course. This also has the advantage of your being able to communicate more directly with Juan. And then you'd also have friends you know well near by (María Luisa, Magda, etc. . . .) who can help solve problems as they arise and save you having to go from place to place for help. As for next year, we'll have to think about that . . . Is this okay with you? I'm writing now to suggest this to Alfonso. I'm beginning to be concerned about your studies. As you know, I don't mean that in the conventional sense of just getting a degree; I feel it's important for you to be doing something that will really help you in your personal development. It would be good to study sociology in Paris – remember what splendid things we heard about that course? – but you don't speak French. Suppose you begin to study it now, with that in mind? I don't think it would be hard to carry on with that in Rome, but of course you're doing two courses already. Did you know that *Jesus Christ Superstar* ('They'll never let us see *that* in Spain,' everyone said) is now advertised everywhere in Madrid? Of course I shan't be able to see it, and I think you're probably right that there's nothing very special about it. But it must be rather beautiful visually, I think. I congratulate you on your reading! How go the notes on *Luces de Bohemia*? I notice you've given up the idea of the play; what are you writing instead? Or have you some different plan in view? I find that whole subject of *imagination* quite fascinating! I'm making a few notes too, and I've sent some of them to Alfonso. I really miss being able to exchange ideas directly with all of you, especially at this moment when there are so many things to think about, and we could get such a lot out of talking and combining our thoughts. I long for all five of us to be together, working together, from our very varied standpoints, to resolve our problems ... I hope you won't misunderstand what I'm saying – I know you won't – you know too well what I think about this, and about how the traditional family is the source of so many evils that it has got to be destroyed. What I want is for us to get together to exchange feelings and ideas, and thus enriched, we can again go off and each 'do our own thing'. That's the freedom I'm longing for: we were together freely, and we were free to separate when we wanted to. Aren't I right, Juan? Because, as you put it so well, Pablo, '*they* have separated us when it wasn't *our* wish'. That's why I rebel, and shall continue to rebel against this situation, and dream of the time when we get back something of our life as a unit, as what we call a family (though I don't suppose it can ever be what it was before). By the way, talking of dreams, I must tell you that – quite apart from my daydreams! – I'm having the most complicated and sometimes really lovely dreams at night. I decided I should write them down – as you know I've always been that way inclined; and some day when in the mood I'll type them out and send them to you. Some of them are really wonderful, but if I set out to tell you them now, I'd waste a whole priceless half-page – a luxury I simply can't afford. One point for Juan: I read in a Cuban film magazine that they are in the process of publishing the complete works of Eisenstein – apparently he wrote a great many analytical works – I hadn't realized that. I also read with much excitement – because it seems like a marvellous project, though a herculean one that would need an outstanding talent (he would have been the ideal man) – that he wanted to put *Capital* on the screen, and he even went as far as to present part of the outline or scenario. Could you get hold of any of this if it *has* come out? I get a very strange feeling when I write to you now – it's really beginning to worry me the way I'm not getting letters from you. I feel the need for more exchange, for the renewed stimulus I get from what you say to me. As time goes on (though I know why it is, and I'm not anxious about *you* when your letters don't arrive) I start to feel as though my letters to you are a kind of monologue, and I hardly know what to talk about (which is extraordinary, if you think of the *amount* of interests and feelings we have in common!). There's something a bit frightening about such a long separation, without any really fluent communication … There are *so many* questions I want to ask about this fantastic experience you're going through. What problems do you have in a general way? What things concern you most, and what are the difficulties that arise in life *inside* the revolution? What are your specific problems as a future doctor? There are a few books I'd like to send you … I was delighted by your long letter; it's great to see that you're still so lively, and that you're somehow finding time to read, and write, and even to draw. You must be sure to keep using your imagination all the time: it is like a kind of lantern that lights up the darkest places, and makes one able to open up new paths in areas where further progress had seemed an impossibility. Don't let all that work get on top of you. Working at something liberating and enjoyable is a tremendous achievement, but it can become negative if there are no limits at all – try to keep a balance. Are you seeing Pepe and Anisia? You told me they had written to Eva. When, oh when, will our courier come with the letters – he's certainly taking his time! It's getting light – it's now seven-thirty – as I finish this letter. The single bird that was making such a lot of noise a few days ago above the window in our Yeserías courtyard has now been transformed into a large family, chirping much more faintly – but with *great* energy – from all directions. There must be a nest hidden somewhere about here. I've often said that February is the month of spring – my internal spring, that is – but it's evidently the same for a lot of other creatures ... The days are lengthening out, and winter's almost over. How much longer will this separation go on? Not much longer, I'm sure, Mafalda darling. Let's see your smile and your bright eyes! I'll tickle you next week, and then you'll have to laugh ... All my love,

EVA

Letter from Mari Luz Fernández, schoolteacher, aged twenty-five, to her lawyer, Miguel de Castells Arteche. She was arrested by the police in Madrid, and spent 114 days in solitary confinement.

For the first time since I was arrested (five months ago), I am now feeling able to express myself without too much difficulty. For three and a half months I had a great many interesting ideas and impressions to set down, but it was impossible because I didn't have the wherewithal to do it. After I emerged from solitary confinement, the impossibility arose out of the extreme sense of dislocation between my life as it was before and as it is now, and the difficulty of adapting myself to these new circumstances. It was all so *terrible* during my time alone ... What I'm going through now is a reaction, and, especially in the past few days I've felt – felt, or am feeling? (though in fact it is now night-time and my friends are still asleep and I am finding it a bit easier to express myself) – very restricted in what I can express; orally: I stammer, and find it hard to get the words right, etc.; and the same in writing: I repeat words, and find it impossible to get my ideas into any sort of shape ... There can be no doubt that all these problems have arisen from the length of time I had to be totally inactive, and therefore was making almost no purposeful mental effort. Though I felt pretty strong at the beginning, I found certain confusions arising in my mind later on – problems only to be expected in such a situation. Some of the other women who, though to a lesser degree, suffered the same problem of isolation, have cheered me by telling me that it's absolutely normal – in fact it's actually a good sign for these problems to appear at this time.

I have spent the past few days almost completely in bed (a minor stomach upset), and I think that has helped me to recover physically (because I'd really come to feel very tired indeed latterly) as well as psychologically. I hope these days of rest will make me strong enough to get going on some serious study, and a bit of writing. The fact is that up to now I haven't been able to concentrate enough for that – the most I've been able to manage is short periods of reading.

It seems incredible to have been able to write as much as this today, and do it so easily. I'm getting better. Everything will be all right!

Warmest greetings,
MARI LUZ

Eva Forest's letter to Pablo of 19 November 1974 was received from her family just before this edition went to press. It was translated at Penguin Books.

19 November 1974

Darling Pablo,

Your sweet letter touches me so deeply, little comrade of my soul. It's gentle and tender like the autumn light which you miss so much and which makes you think of Yaya and of me. I am going to close my eyes and imagine we are in Miraflores on one of those coldish mornings. You ask me, as you have asked me so many times, to go for a walk with you to talk about life and the problems which are troubling you. Thank you for making me think yet again about the concrete, about reality. Here we are coming to the top, on the road to Canencia and down there's the village and the lakes and in the distance we can see the mist over Madrid. Your reply to that girl's interpretation of your position seems to be absolutely correct. It represents an enormous step forward, a real lesson for the traditional, bourgeois method of explaining events. Let me explain. This person comes from the world of psychoanalysis. Years ago, thanks to his profound and analytical powers of perception, the great Freud discovered that so many things go on in the human brain that many of them never reach the surface, but stay buried in the subconscious, working away in the dark. So it is a sort of hidden motor which conditions everything that people do – how they act, react, burst out of themselves and turn in on themselves. With the discovery of how and why the mechanisms work in the way they do, human beings are able to understand their actions much more clearly and can even control them. Right from birth, man is a sort of soft material where everything leaves its mark. Each mark is a link in the whole process which determines his development: everything influences everything else, man influences his environment and in turn his environment influences him. Freud's great discovery in his time was the creative potential of the forces of the instinct when these are allowed to roam free and how paralysis or 'neurosis' sets in when this energy is repressed in any one of a thousand possible ways. This represented a great discovery at that time. By now, it should have been integrated, taken up, surpassed by applying dialectical negation to the process of scientific investigation (just as Marx, who was a great admirer and student of Hegel's work, uses this method to negate Hegel). It should have gone forward. Unfortunately the psychoanalysts of today are not usually up to the level of the master. Or else they stop there, letting his living thought atrophy, dogmatizing and paralysing his work or just skimming its surface without getting any useful experience from it. Both are superficial, unscientific ways of approaching problems. Your reply is absolutely right. It is stunningly correct to say that *we have not left each other* but that THEY HAVE SEPARATED US, when what you want and what we want is to be together. I cannot find a better answer because yours underlines the huge gulf between two concepts: the individualist one which relies on sensory perception (where sensation dominates and the phenomenon is accounted for on the emotional plane only) and the other which is open, conscious of Mankind and its history. This one is the total interpretation which allows for data other than the purely subjective to be taken into account. There is no danger that you will ever feel this rejection, precisely because you have always been aware of what was happening to us all and when feelings of sadness, of anger, of love came over you you already were prepared by a prior historical understanding. Do you see how everything we learn becomes useful sooner or later? Don't you think that those theses of Mao which you once read are proving their usefulness now? Or even a conversation which you and I once had somewhere? This gulf between you and your friend demonstrates just how correct our interpretation of the world is. What for her was an enclosed situation, something which 'scars one for life' like a stigma or a sentence, for us is an open-ended tragedy, one which is tremendously sad, but is the result of a specific determinate situation in a determinate historical context which can be explained and which does not dominate us, for we know it, we think about it, and we overcome it. So where a bourgeois interpretation would operate in terms of a separation and a breach, we believe ourselves today to be more united than ever, stronger than ever, and although we may appear to have nothing, we are millionaires of love, of brotherhood and innumerable other things? ... Dear Pablo while we've been talking away, we've almost got to the port and we should go back home for lunch. Now we have come down the hill and I ask you 'How is M— and her family?' As I still haven't received the first letter which you sent to us from Rome, I haven't any information at all. It is inevitable that although you know it is better for you to be outside Spain you should feel pain at having to go. But nothing will change. Friends are not lost in a day, and when you come back everything will be much better. What is important now is that you should be getting rich experiences out of all this, that you should live, see, feel and reflect. Haven't you tried to draw again like you used to in Madrid? You wrote to me from Genoa, that means that you are travelling, seeing places. I remember two things about Genoa which made a big impression on me. I was twenty-four years old and had just finished my degree. A group of us went in by car. We were almost broke so we ate spaghetti all the time. I remember a very big port with a district which reminded me of the Chinese quarter in Barcelona and I remember a cemetery (renowned for its sculpture) which I didn't like one bit. I imagine you being very much loved by everybody, going to the theatre, seeing people, having to answer their questions. I know very well that you are so different from Juan, that you are capable of spending hours in the corner of a room somewhere reading and writing. But it is important to keep in contact with people you know. When one knows, as you do, how to 'look', then there are things to be learnt in all kinds of people and all kinds of places. Dear Pablo, with this long walk (how short it seems to me) I have forgotten to tell you that they have made a new charge against me in the last few days, which implicates me in the death of Carrero Blanco. Some newspaper reported that I cried when I heard the news. It's not true; it didn't even surprise me that much. What I did experience was a sort of transposition of historical time: I felt as though I was taking part in one of those trials of the Middle Ages. I couldn't stop myself thinking of Miguel Servetus being taken through the streets of Geneva and of a thousand other things like that and then when I realized that this was all happening in the twentieth century I saw that it was quite understandable if one makes a scientific analysis of history. I am not sad. Sometimes tears come into my eyes, but they are tears of anger and impotence. And then I think how many comrades are suffering even greater injustices and I feel like their little sister so I pull myself together and I think how lucky I am to have realized in time, to know that we must fight so that one day human beings will be free to realize their potential. And then I have faith that things will be sorted out and the truth will shine out and that then nobody, nobody at all will be able to separate us.

Looking back over your letter, I accept with respect what you say about your silence. You are right. If you feel the need to maintain your privacy, then you must do so. I only want to make you aware of the possibility that the problem which we try to keep to ourselves sometimes bursts out where it's least expected. But when it is really necessary to keep quiet and one knows that is the right thing to do, then O K. I suppose that M— will have received the card I sent her, anyway I'd like you to let me know. Alfonso tells me that he is going to send you some poems that he has written. He also says that the book *I see you Vietnam* is coming out soon. Can you send me a copy? My lawyer tells me that he had a very nice letter from you and that he has replied to you. Well, young Paulus, here we are coming into the village, it will soon be time for lunch, we'll lay the table, Eva will be late, as always, because she'll have been with Pacita, and Alfonso will tell a joke and then put on the radio. We are the same family as ever. Life goes on, rich with experiences, full of promise for the future Don't you think that we're incredibly lucky to have been chosen to go through it together, with a companion as wise as Alfonso, with such an intelligent Mafaldita, and with a veritable Vietnamese of a Juan? There are even some moments of happiness in this imprisonment of mine...! I love you so much ...

EVA